CRICUT
2 BOOKS IN 1

Cricut For Beginners +
Cricut Project Ideas

Master Cricut Design Space as an expert and let your Creativity run wild with lots of unique Project Ideas!

Melissa Maker

Disclaimer

All erudition contained in this book is given for informational and educational purposes only. The author is not in any way accountable for any results or outcomes that emanate from using this material. Constructive attempts have been made to provide information that is both accurate and effective, but the author is not bound for the accuracy or use/misuse of this information.

Table of Contents

CRICUT FOR BEGINNERS............................7

INTRODUCTION...8

The Different Cricut Models.....................10

What Projects Can You Do with a Cricut Machine?...13

Tools and Accessories Needed When Using a Cricut Machine...15

Materials that Cricut Machines Can Cut Through...23

CHAPTER ONE...25

Setting Up Your Cricut Machine...............25

Tools Needed...26

Step-By-Step Process..........................27

CHAPTER TWO..32

Everything You Need To Know About Cricut Design Space..32

Cricut Design Space Canvas Area..........33

Cricut Design Space Tricks...................52

CHAPTER THREE..54

Cricut Access Subscription.....................54

Frequent Cricut Problems and Solutions..58

CHAPTER FOUR...69

Maintaining Cricut..................................69

Maintaining the Cricut Machine..............69

Maintaining the Cricut Cutting Mat.........73

Maintaining the Cricut Cutting Blade.......78

CHAPTER FIVE..81

Cricut Model Comparison.......................81

Cricut Explore One.............................81

Cricut Explore Air.............................85

Cricut Explore Air 2...........................88

Cricut Maker 91

Which Cricut Model Should You Use?......95

CHAPTER SIX 97

Frequently Asked Questions....................97

Questions on Cricut Design Space..........98

Questions on all Cricut Machines.........103

CONCLUSION 107

Simple Projects to Start With 108

General Tips for Beginners.................110

CRICUT PROJECT IDEAS.....................113

INTRODUCTION..............................116

Models......................................118

Accessories 121

Tools 124

Materials To Use 136

Where To Find Materials.....................139

CHAPTER ONE 141

Setting Up The Machine 141

CHAPTER TWO 149

Project Ideas By Craft.......................149

Paper Crafts................................149

Adhesive Vinyl Crafts 150

Iron-On Vinyl Crafts 151

Wood Crafts 152

Fabric Crafts 152

CHAPTER THREE 154

Step-By-Step Guide on Some Cricut
Projects 154

Felt Roses 155

Custom Coasters 157

Customized Doormat......................... 160

T-Shirts (Vinyl, Iron On) 162

3d Paper Flowers (Paper).................... 166

Luminaries 168

Shamrock Earrings............................ 170

Valentine's Day Classroom Cards 173

Glitter And Felt Hair Bow Supplies........ 175

Halloween T-Shirt 177

Hand Lettered Cake Topper................. 180

Unicorn Free Printable 182

Custom Back To School Supplies.......... 184

CHAPTER FOUR 187

TIPS AND TECHINQUES 187

Design Canvas Platform...................... 189

Cut Screen Platform 198

CONCLUSION 208

CRICUT FOR BEGINNERS

Step By Step Guide To Start Cricut. Master Cricut Design Space to Easily Create Unique and Original Project.

Melissa Maker

INTRODUCTION

You've probably heard about Cricut from your friends, or you have a Cricut machine sitting at home, which was given to you as a gift, and you're not sure where to start from. But, not to worry, because you've picked the right guide for beginners.

Photo credit- cricut.com

People who are into crafts and do-it-yourself designs all around the world are very familiar with Cricut and their innovative cutting machines. Cricut is the most popular brand name for die-cutting machines, also called cutting plotters or craft plotter machines. It can be used for simple projects like scrapbooking or very elaborate projects like making Christmas decorations.

The well-known brand is made by Provo Craft & Novelty, Inc. of Spanish Fork, Utah. The brand, apart from making home die-cutting machines, manufacturers, crafts, arts, and merchandise.

The home die-cutting machines are meant for cutting paper, vinyl, fabric, and over a hundred other materials that we will explore in this guide.

A Cricut machine can be likened to a printer, especially because of the design. But, the Cricut machine won't print out your design. Instead, it will cut the design out from the material you're using! So, you can make a design on your computer, and the machine will cut it out of fabric, paper, cardboard, vinyl, and even the most unlikely materials. When using some Cricut models, you can print out your design on whatever material of your choosing.

The Different Cricut Models

The models that we will look at here are those that are well-suited with the recent Cricut Design Space application.

- **Cricut Maker**

This is what Cricut refers to as its most flexible smart cutting machine. The machine line was released on the 20th of August 2017. The Cricut Maker series is also unique from the other models because it provides a rotary blade that can directly cut through the fabric.

Photo credit- amazon.com

They are created to cut through thicker materials than the other models. They can cut through felt, basswood, balsa wood, leather, and non-bonded fabric, as well as all the different materials that Cricut machines can cut through.

- **Cricut Explore One**

Although the Cricut Explore One machine can cut over sixty materials, including paper and fabric, it cannot cut the kind of materials that the Cricut Maker cuts.

Photo credit- amazon.com

The machine is wired, but if you want to connect it to Bluetooth, you can easily purchase a wireless Bluetooth adapter separately.

Unlike the other models, the Cricut Explore One has one tool slot.

- **Cricut Explore Air**

Next, we have the Cricut Explore Air, which is a wireless model. The model can also cut through the materials that the Explore One can cut through. The difference between them is in the design and the increase in power.

- **Cricut Explore Air 2**

The Cricut Explore 2 is an upgrade of the Explore Air. It added three colors to the line, which are Rose Anna, Mint Blue, and Giffin Lilac. The updated model also had a Fast Mode to cut materials like vinyl. It features card stock at up to double the speeds of the other models.

Photo credit- amazon.com

Cricut usually refers to this model as its DIY speed machine.

What Projects Can You Do with a Cricut Machine?

Photo credit- inkleinedtostamp.com

We cannot mention all the projects that you can do with a Cricut machine because they are so many. But, for all the creative minds going into the guide, here are some of the popular projects that you can do with a Cricut machine.

- Creating handmade, custom cards
- Cutting out letters or shapes for scrapbooking.
- Addressing an envelope.
- Creating leather bracelets.
- Designing and creating decorations or buntings for parties.
- Designing and creating Christmas decorations and ornaments.
- Designing t-shirts or other fabrics.
- Making painting stencils.
- Creating vinyl stickers.
- Creating labels.
- Designing and creating symbolic pillows.
- Inscription of designs on plates, cups, tumblers, or mugs.
- Engraving designs on glass.

- Creating decorations and stickers for your walls.
- Creating designs on wood or wooden signs.

Photo credit- inspiration.cricut.com

- Cutting fabric pieces to sow on another fabric or quilt squares.
- Creating decorative stickers.
- Creating felt coasters.
- Creating designs on water bottles.
- Designing and creating customized tote bags.

Tools and Accessories Needed When Using a Cricut Machine

You can't possibly use a Cricut machine alone, but the type of accessories or tools that you need depend on the kind of project that you're using the machine for. If you're going into home décor, you'll need different tools from those going into paper crafts.

Necessities

Irrespective of any project, some necessary accessories are essential. Some of these accessories come with Cricut, while some can be purchased from Cricut.

- **Cutting Mats**

Cutting mats come in three kinds, which are strong grip, standard grip, and light grip. You can also purchase any one of the sizes that they come in, which is either the 12 inches by 24 inches or the 12 inches by 12 inches mat.

Photo credit- amazon.com

The strong grip mat is ideal when you're cutting stiffened fabric, glitter cardstock, chipboard, specialty cardstock, and other thick materials. For thinner materials like embossed cardstock or standard cardstock, vinyl, pattern paper, or iron-on, we recommend the standard grip mat. For the lightest materials, the light grip mat is needed. Light materials include light cardstock, office paper, vellum, or other materials.

A newly bought Cricut machine includes a cutting mat in the box, and so you don't have to buy a mat separately. After a while, the mat will lose its stickiness and you can either apply glue to maintain it or buy a new one.

Also, when considering your project, you should get the right mat. If your mat is light grip and you try to cut a thick fabric, you might end up messing the entire project up because the material will keep on shifting from the mat.

- **Cutting Blades**

Cutting Blades are the essential accessories needed when using Cricut. After all, you can't cut without a blade.

Photo credit- amazon.com

Cutting blades also come in three types. First, we have the standard blade that usually accompanies the Cricut machine. The blade is very sharp and strong, but after a while, you will need to change the blade when it becomes blunt. So, you should have extra blades on hand just in case.

Photo credit- amazon.com

Next, we have the German carbide blade. You can easily purchase this from Cricut too. It's stronger than the standard blade, and it is created to cut through mid-weight materials. The blade also lasts for a longer time and doesn't easily break.

Lastly, designed for very thick materials, we have the deep cut blade. The deep cut blade is meant for cutting materials that go with the strong grip cutting mat. You can also use the blade to cut materials like stamp material, magnet, and some other fabrics.

- **Spatula and Scraper**

Not many people bother with purchasing a spatula and scraper when they want to use their Cricut machine. But these tools are useful when it comes to taking materials off the cutting mat.

For the spatula, you can use it to remove the material from the mat without damaging the material. It provides accuracy. In the case of the scraper, you will need to maintain the mat by cleaning it. This tool is helpful with scraping off leftover materials on the mat and cleaning it. This keeps the machine durable and it will last for a long time. Also, when you want to start on a new project, you can quickly use the mat without having to clean it.

Apart from these essential tools, for specific types of projects, some devices are crucial when working on those projects.

Vinyl or Iron-On

For example, when working on vinyl or iron-on projects, they both use the same type of tools because they are both similar. Iron-on plans are pretty much heat transfer vinyl projects.

You can use vinyl to decorate tumblers, cups, or mugs; create decals for frames or walls and other projects. Iron-on is used to decorate fabric like adding designs on t-shirts.

- **Transfer Tape**

Circuit also manufactures this tool, and it is entirely transparent. This way, when transferring or placing your vinyl project, you can see it easily and handle it more carefully.

- **Weeder**

When carrying out vinyl or iron-on project, a weeder is crucial because it can be used to single out tiny pieces that are on your project like the pieces of vinyl that aren't being used from the backing sheet.

Paper

Apart from vinyl projects, paper projects are probably the most popular projects that most crafters carry out. When using Cricut, most people start with paper projects because they are light and relatively more comfortable to do.

You can use paper to create shapes, numbers, letters, cards, envelopes, banners, decorations, stickers, and more. For paper projects, there are two general tools that you will possibly need.

- **Pens**

When using any of the Cricut Explore machines, you can quickly write out your designs. When you want to draw, Cricut provides some free fonts and some fonts that you can buy from Cricut Access. Also, if you have fonts on your computer, you can use that too.

Photo credit- amazon.com

You can buy different pens from Cricut that are compatible with any of the Explore machines. Their types of pens include calligraphy pens, fine tip pens, gold pens, metallic pens, and pens of a wide range of colors. Although you can use other pens, Cricut machines work best with Cricut pens.

The great thing about Cricut machines is that they provide for two slots so that you can use the pen and the blade simultaneously. This allows for quick designing and cutting instantaneously.

- **Scoring Tool**

This is also called a scoring stylus, and it is used for folding lines on boxes, envelops, cards, or any other papers. The same way you can design or draw and cut at the same time, you can also install the scoring tool in the machine when the blade is already installed.

This makes your designing process fast and easy.

Additional Tools

Apart from the usual design tools, you can also purchase some tools that make using the Cricut machine more convenient. Depending on the project you are using, these tools might be handy.

- **Tool Kit**

Instead of purchasing your tools one-by-one, some people go for the economical option and buy a tool kit instead. A standard tool kit should include scissors, weeders, scrapers, spatulas, and tweezers. If you're going into iron-on or vinyl projects, then you should probably purchase this type of tool kit.

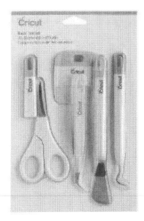

Photo credit- amazon.com

Some advanced tool kits add a paper trimmer and scoring stylus. This tool kit is excellent for those interested in paper projects.

- **Bluetooth Adapter**

As stated earlier, Cricut Explore One does not come with an inbuilt Bluetooth adapter. If you want to use this model, you can buy a Bluetooth adapter from Cricut. This way, you can easily use your Cricut wherever your computer, laptop, or iPad is.

Materials that Cricut Machines Can Cut Through

Cricut machines, in general, can cut through over a hundred materials. Of course, we can't mention them all, but we will categorize them into six categories.

- Paper and cardstock- this includes about 35 types of paper and cardstock.
- Fabrics- including about 16 types of fabrics and textiles.
- Iron-On- which includes about six types of iron-on materials.
- Vinyl- which includes about ten types of vinyl materials.
- Additional Materials- ranging from adhesive foil and adhesive wood to washi sheets and temporary tattoo paper, Cricut can cut them all.
- Cricut Maker Special- this particular model of Cricut can cut through materials that the others can't like chiffon, cashmere, terry cloth, knits, jersey, velvet, tweed, and others.

Photo credit- almostpractical.com

Now that we've explored the basic introduction of Cricut and its usefulness, we will move on to the intricacies of using Cricut for any craft and design that you are interested in.

Thank you for choosing this book! If you enjoy reading this book, I will be looking forward to seeing your review on Amazon. I'd like to know what you think!

With this guide, any beginner planning on expanding their creativity with Cricut will be able to do anything with the Cricut Design Space and also use the best and updated Cricut machines out there.

CHAPTER ONE

Setting Up Your Cricut Machine

Setting up your Cricut machine is more like unwrapping a Christmas present! You have to be careful, but at the same time, you're eager to get started with it.

Photo credit: ourdesignspace.com

The machine setup of any Cricut machine won't take you more than an hour, and there are a few tools that come with the Cricut machine to guide your installation.

Here, we will be using the Cricut Maker to explain the machine setup seeing as it is the newest Cricut technology available.

Tools Needed

- Cricut Maker.
- Power cord and USB cable.
- Fine point pen.
- A fine point blade.
- Rotatory blade with housing.
- LightGrip Mat 12" by 12".
- FabricGrip Mat 12" by 12".
- A computer, tablet, or mobile phone which is connected to the internet.

All these tools, except the computer or mobile device, come in the box with the Cricut Maker.

Step-By-Step Process

1. Opening the Box

When you purchase a bundle from Cricut, you will receive a few boxes, but the most significant box amongst them will hold the Cricut Maker. To recognize it, you'll see the picture of the Maker on the box.

Photo credit: amazon.com

When opening the Cricut box, the first thing you see is the welcome packet placed on the machine. The welcome package contains a welcome book, a rotary blade with cover, a fine point pen, a USB cable, and a packet with your first project.

When you take the Cricut machine out of the box, the power cord will be underneath along with the cutting mats.

2. Unwrapping

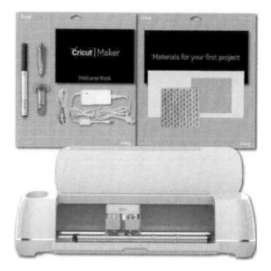

Photo credit: craft-e-corner.com

The Cricut machine is wrapped with a layer of cellophane and a protective wrapper. Before setting up the device, you have to remove the wrappings.

Some Styrofoam protects the in-housing of the machine, and that has to go too.

Your Cricut Maker will also come with some supplies, and you should unwrap them and check them out. Lucky for you, the fine point blade is already installed in the Cricut Maker, so you don't have to bother with that.

3. Visit cricut.com/setup

The next step in setting up your machine lies in the technical aspects. Cricut has a webpage dedicated to walking you through this process, which makes it super easy.

Open cricut.com/setup on your device. You can use any device that is compatible with Cricut like a smartphone, tablet or computer. When you do that, you will be asked to install Cricut Design Space and also sign up. Then, you'll be given your Cricut ID.

If you have been using a former Cricut machine before, then you can carry on with your previous ID.

4. Plugging It In

Next, you need to take your USB cord and the power cord to power up your Cricut machine.

This will be shown on the setup wizard of the webpage.

Photo credit: happilyeverafteretc.com

For the USB cord, you connect the square end to the Cricut Maker device and the other end to the computer. And, the power cord is easy to connect the Cricut Maker to the power outlet.

5. Claim Your Bonus

After plugging in your Cricut, you will be able to claim a free welcome bonus from Cricut, which is a free month of Cricut Access. This means that you get to enjoy access to projects, fonts, and Cricut Cut Files.

6. Begin Your Project

If you need a little something to practice with before starting on your intended project, Cricut Maker machines usually come with a little project in the welcome pack to help you get acquainted with the tools.

The Maker comes with all the tools that you need to complete the project, which is usually the task of making a little card.

After this, then you can begin using it. The thing is, when you want to use your Cricut Maker, you need to learn how to use Cricut Design Space.

CHAPTER TWO

Everything You Need To Know About Cricut Design Space

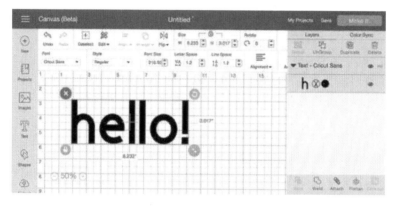

Photo credit: inspiration.cricut.com

Cricut Beginners usually get discouraged when they open Cricut Design Space.

This is because, there are a lot of icons and options that you need to learn. If you don't, you can even spoil a project with the wrong decision.

But, once you understand what all the panels and icons are meant for, it will be easy to jump into a new project with confidence.

This chapter will teach you all you need to know about Cricut Design Space so that you can get the best out of your Cricut machine.

Cricut Design Space Canvas Area

Before you cut up your projects, the Canvas area is where all the designing and arts happen. Here, you can organize your project, upload images or fonts.

The Cricut Design Space is just similar to the other design programs that most of us are useful, like Adobe Creative Cloud, Photoshop, or Illustrator. And so, if you have any experience with these programs, then it won't be difficult for you to understand the Design Space.

There is also the choice of getting a Cricut Access membership which will be explained later. With this, you can create your designs and let your creativity flow.

So, the Canvas Area is where you edit and touch up your designs before cutting them, but because there are many options that might overwhelm you, we will be taking these options one-by-one to explain their uses.

The Canvas Area is made up of the Right Panel, Left Panel, Top Panel, and Canvas Area.

1. **Right Panel**

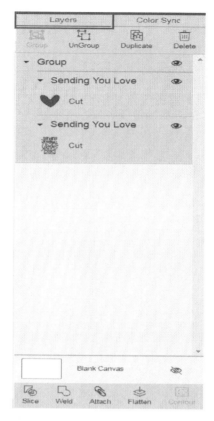

Photo credit: help.cricut.com

The Right Panel deals with layers, and so it can also be called the Layers Panel. Layers signify the designs that are on the canvas area. The number of layers that you use depends on the complexity of your design or the project that you're working on.

When making a birthday card, you will have texts and different decorations, and probably a picture or two. All of these are the layers of the design.

This panel allows you to create and manage layers when making a design. Every item that is on the layers panel will display the Fill or Line type that you are using.

- *Group, Ungroup, Duplicate, and Delete.*

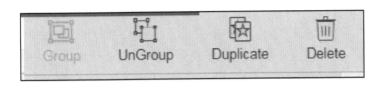

These settings allow you to move different designs around the canvas area.

- Group: This allows you to group layers. When you have different layers that come together to make a complicated design, you use this option to bring them together. For example, if you're making a house, there will be different parts of that house. A standard home will have a roof, door, walls, and windows. 'Group' allows you to arrange all the layers and ensure that they stay together when you're making a design.
- Ungroup: You can also separate a design of different layers, by clicking on this button. This is pretty much the opposite of 'Group'.
- Duplicate: As the name implies, this option will duplicate the layers that you select on the canvas.
- Delete: This option will delete any layer that you select and remove it from the canvas.

- ***Blanck Canvas***

This is also a layer in the Right panel that gives you the option of changing the color of the canvas. If you're experimenting with your design, you can use this option to place it against various backgrounds.

- ***Layer Visibility***

This is represented by a little eye that is on every layer on the panel. It signifies the visibility of that layer or design. During designing, if you see that a particular segment or element doesn't look right, you can click on the eye to hide it. That way, you don't end up deleting it permanently if you decide to put it back. The hidden item can be identified with a cross mark.

- ***Slice, Weld, Attach, Flatten and Contour***

It's important to learn how to use these five tools. No matter what you're designing, they will come in handy.

- Slice: This tool is meant for cutting out texts, shapes, and other elements from a whole design.
- Weld: This is used for combining shapes to make a new shape. If you want to do something different with your designs, you can join two or more shapes together.
- Attach: This is like a more powerful version of the Group option. It connects shapes and changes the color to match whatever background color that you're using. This will remain even after cutting.
- Flatten: This tool is useful when you're about to print two or more shapes. To do this, you should pick the layers that you want to print and select the Flatten option.
- Contour- If you want to hide a layer of design, or just a small part, you can use this option to do so. Although, you can only do this when your design has layers that can be taken apart.
-

- **_Color Sync_**

This option is meant for evening out the colors of your design and even background. You can use this to change different shades of a color to just one color. It synchronizes the colors, as the name implies.

2. **Left Panel**

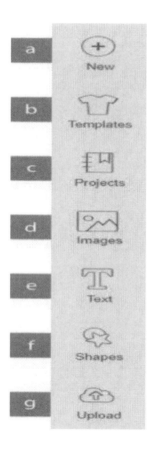

The left panel includes all the options you need for inserting. You can add shapes, texts, images, even ready-to-cut projects.

With this panel, you can add everything that you plan on cutting. The panel has seven options, and we will explore them all.

- **New**

You select this option when you want to create a new page apart from the one that you're using to design.

It's advisable to save your designs before you move to the new page just in case you need it on another time. If not, you can lose your designs.

- **Templates**

A template is used to give you a feel of what your design will look like when you cut it out on a particular type of fabric like a t-shirt or a bag. If you're making an iron-on design on a bag, it will show you a picture of the bag, and you can place the design on the template so you can plan how it will look in real life.

Templates are great because they give you an idea of what your design looks like when cut out. It won't cut out an actual backpack for you.

- ***Projects***

If you're ready to cut, then you should go to projects. You will pick your project, edit it, and tailor it to your tastes and click on the 'Make It' option.

A large number of the project available are available to Cricut Access members, or some are available for purchase. Apart from these, a few are free.

- ***Images***

Images allow you to add a personal touch to your designs. With this option, you can insert pictures provided for you on Cricut Design Space.

Cricut even provides free images every week, although some come with Cricut Access.

- **Text**

The text option allows you to add a text to your design or just on the canvas area. It opens a small window telling you to add text, and so you can do that and customize the font and color.

- **Shapes**

You use this option when you want to add shapes to your canvas area. Cricut Design Space offers some shapes, namely triangle, square, pentagon, hexagon, octagon, star, and heart.
There is also the Score Line tool under the Shapes option. You can use this option to fold the shapes into different shapes, especially when you're making cards.

- **Upload**

The last tool in the Left panel is the Upload tool, which allows you to upload your files and images apart from those Cricut provides for you.
With this, you can upload images or patterns.

3. **Top Panel**

Photo credit: help.cricut.com

The top panel is the busiest panel. It has two different subpanels, and generally, the top panel is used for the general editing and organizing of elements and layers of design.

- ***First Subpanel***

Photo credit: help.cricut.com

This allows you to name your project, save it, and eventually cut it. Here, you can navigate to saving, naming, and sending your project to the Cricut machine for cutting.

- Toggle Menu: This part of the subpanel allows you to manage your account and your account subscriptions. This menu also gives you the option of updating your

Cricut Design Space, calibrating your machine and others.

- Project Name: You can use this to name your project. Your project will be automatically called 'Untitled' until you give it a name that you can use to identify it.
- My Projects: This is a library of all your projects saved on the Cricut Design Space, and so you can always refer to old projects.
- Save: This option saves your project into the library. As you work, you should save in case your browser crashes.
- Cricut Maker / Cricut Explore: When you're using Cricut Design Space for the first time, it asks you if you're using a Cricut Explore machine from the series or a Cricut Maker. Seeing as the Cricut Maker is a more advances machine, it provides more benefits on Design Space than the machines in the Explore series.
- Make It: After uploading your files, you click on Make It so that it can cut. The software will categorize your projects depending on their colors. Also, if you're planning to cut more than one project, you can use this to increase the projects that you want to cut.

- **Second Subpanel**

Photo credit: youtube.com

This subpanel is the editing menu. It allows you to edit, organize, and arrange images and fonts on the Canvas Area.

- Undo & Redo:

You can click undo when you make a mistake or create something that you don't want. And, you can click on redo if you mistakenly delete something that you need.

- Cut under (Line type): All your layers on the canvas area have this line type. After selecting the Make It option, the Cricut machine cuts the designs on your canvas area. Cut under allows you to change the colors of the layers and the fill too.
- Draw (Line type):

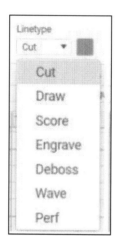

Cricut also allows you to write and draw on your designs. When you select this line type, you're given different options of different Cricut pens, and so, you can use these to draw on the canvas area.

Here, when you click on Make It, your Cricut machine will draw or write instead of cutting.

- Score (Line type): This is an advanced version of the Scoring Line in the left panel. When you select this option for a layer, the layer will look scored. And so, when you click on Make It, the Cricut machine will score the materials instead of cutting it.

When you want to score, you will require a scoring stylus or scoring wheel. The scoring wheel can only work with the Cricut Maker.

- Engrave, Wave, Deboss, and Perf (Line type): These four tools are brand new! They were released by Cricut recently and they can only be used by Cricut Maker users. Also, that user has to have the latest version of the Design Space application. These tools allow you to have significant effects on a lot of materials.
- Fill: This is mainly used for patterns and printing. You can only use this option when Cut is selected as a line type.
- Print:

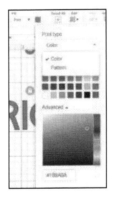

Photo credit: daydreamintoreality.com

Any Cricut user really likes this option. This allows you first print out your design, and then cut them out. To use the print option, when the fill option is active, you first click on Make It. And then, you send the files to your printer at home before feeding it into the Cricut for cutting.

- Edit:

This icon contains three options on the drop-down menu. There is the cut option that allows you to re-move an element from the canvas, the copy option which copies the same component without removing it and the paste option, which inserts the element that was cut or copied.
- Select All: You can use this to highlight everything on your canvas area.
- Align: There are different options under this, and it is important that you master all of them. They are:

Photo credit: daydreamintoreality.com

46

Align Left: This option ensures that all the elements are aligned to the left. The detail at the end of the left side will determine how the other details move.

Center Horizontally: This will align all the elements horizontally.

Align Right: This will align the elements to the right. As with align left, the item at the end of the left side will determine how the other items move.

Align Top: This will align the elements you select to the top of the canvas page.

Center Vertically: This will align all the design elements vertically.

Align Bottom: This does the opposite of the Align Top option by aligning the layers or elements to the bottom.

Center: This aligns both the horizontally aligned and vertically aligned elements to the center.

- Distribute: This allows you to create the same spacing between elements or layers.

Distribute Horizontally

Distribute Vertically

- Flip:

If you want to reflect your designs as though they are looking at a mirror, you can use this option. It provides two options.

Flip Horizontal

Flip Vertical

- Arrange:

The arrange options allow you to move elements like images, texts, or designs to the front or back of others. It provides four options.

Send to Back: This will displace the selected designs or elements and take them to the back.

Move Backward: If you select an element and click on this, the elements moves back once. If you have three parts, you can move one to the middle of the other two.

Move Forward: this is the opposite and it moves the element forward once.

Send to Front: This will displace the selected element and take it to the front.

- Size:

This provides you with the options to adjust, increase or decrease the size of the elements or total design. Everything that you create has a scale, and you use this to modify the size. This is especially if you have a specific format that you're following.

- Rotate:

The Cricut Design Space allows you to rotate the element or layer to any angle that you choose.

- Position:

Seeing as the canvas area has grid lines, you can use these options to pick a particular position for the element on the X and Y axis.

- Font:

For your projects, Cricut provides you with different fonts if you're using Cricut Access. If not, you can use your system's font or use the Cricut fonts for a price.

- Font Size: This allows you to increase or decrease the size of your font.
- Line Space: This is especially useful when you want to ensure that your texts on your design are evenly spaced or spaced according to your preference.
- Letter Space: This allows you to arrange the spaces between the letters.

- Style:

This includes Regular, which is the default setting. Bold, which makes the font thick. Italic, which tilts the font sideways. Bold Italic which combines both the Bold and Italic function.

- Curve:

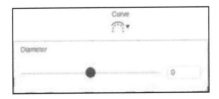

Photo credit: daydreamintoreality.com

You can also design your texts by using the curve setting. You can curve your text upwards or inwards. You can also curve your texts into a circle.
- Advanced:

On the top editing panel, this is the last option.
Ungroup to Letters: This allows you to disconnect each letter into single layers each.
Ungroup to Lines: This allows you to disconnect a paragraph on different lines.
Ungroup to Layers: This is a very tricky option, and it's only available on Cricut Access or if you purchase it.

4. Canvas Area

This is the main workspace of the Cricut Design Space. Here, you have all the elements and designs that you're working on.

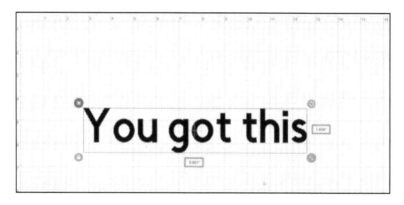

Photo credit: youtube.com

- **Canvas Grid and Dimensions**

Grid lines cover your canvas area on the Cricut Design Space and separate the area into small squares. The canvas area looks like the cutting mat, so you will feel like you're designing on your cutting mat on the screen.

You can use inches or centimeters, and you can turn off the grid in your settings.

- **Zoom Out or In**

You can use this to zoom in or out on your canvas area. If you want to make a design bigger so you can work on it, or just an element, you can use this option.

- **Selection**

When you select a layer or more, the selection color is blue, and four corners around it allow you to modify the layer. There is an X that is colored red; you click on this when you want to delete the layers.

Cricut Design Space Tricks

- Search Items:

When searching for images, firstly, leave out the 's'. If you're searching for Heart shapes, you should search for 'Heart' instead of 'Hearts.' When you remove the 's,' you get more results.

Also, if you can't find a particular image, you should search for the synonym of the picture. Case in point, when making a Valentine's card, search for flower, heart, love, etc.

- Get Free Stuff:

If you want to get free images in the Design Space Image library, use the filter and click on the free option. This will present all the free photos to you.

Photo credit: craft-e-corner.com

You can also get free fonts. You can download free fonts from Font Squirrel and use them when designing on Cricut.

With all of this information, rest assured that you're no longer a beginner when it comes to Cricut Design Space.

CHAPTER THREE

Cricut Access Subscription

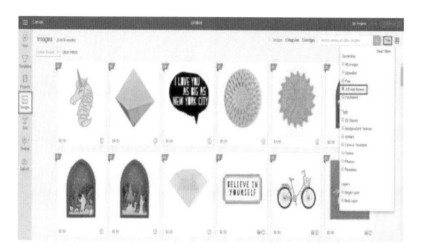

Photo credit: help.cricut.com

In this guide, you might have heard about the Cricut Access Subscription a few times and also all the benefits that the members enjoy. You might also wonder if the subscription is worth it.

Cricut Access can be referred to as a paid membership for Cricut members. It gives its members instant and unlimited access to an incredible library to help them design and create projects. The library has over 90,000 images, over a hundred fonts, and many ready-to-cut projects.

It is advisable that you should only use Cricut Access if you're planning on going in-depth with your designs on Cricut Design Space. It's a really cool deal because you get a lot of fonts, images and projects.

There is a simple contrast between Cricut Access and Cricut Design Space. Firstly, Design Space is completely free. With Design Space, you are allowed to upload designs, touch them up and cut them with the machine.

Photo credit: help.cricut.com

On the other hand, Cricut Access is not free but you have to pay to use it by choosing one of their plans. The designs, fonts, photos and projects are given to you once you've paid and you then use them in the Design Space application.

If you're not a Cricut Access member, that doesn't mean that you will not be able to see the fonts, designs or photos that are seemingly exclusive to Cricut Access. You can still use them, but you will have to pay for it before cutting it out.

Cricut Access Plans

Generally, all Cricut Access plans provide the following:

- Over 400 fonts for your unlimited use.

- Unlimited use of over 50,000 images, ready-to-cut projects, and graphics.

- 10% savings on cartridges, images, and ready-to-cut projects and fonts from known brands like Hello Kitty, Disney, and others.

- 10% savings on any of the physical products and merchandise that you purchase on their website.

- You also get Priority Member Care Line, which means that you get half the wait time that others get.

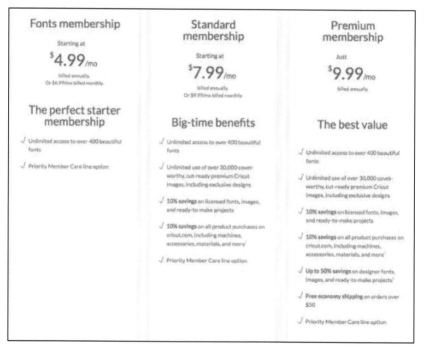

Photo credit: inspiration.cricut.com

Cricut has three plans which are highly convenient and provide you with a lot of benefits.

- **Perfect Starter Plan**

If you're not sure about using Cricut Access, this is the best plan to test it and see if it's something that you need. It provides you with all the benefits mentioned above, and it costs about $10 monthly.

- **Annual Plan**

The Perfect Starter plan and the Annual plan are almost the same. The difference between them both is that, while Perfect Starter is a monthly subscription, this is annual. Here, you make a one-year commitment, and you pay $95.88 yearly. This is $7.99 monthly.

- **Premium Plan**

Apart from the benefits I mentioned above, you also get a lot more discounts with the Premium plan. You get 50% off on licensed graphics, fonts, and ready-to-cut projects. You also get free economy shipping when you purchase goods worth more than $50.

This is also an annual plan which costs $119.88 yearly. This translates to $9.99 monthly.

Do you need Cricut Access?

If you create your designs, illustrations, and projects, then you don't need Cricut Access.

But, if you're looking for free and even paid ideas on the internet without stress, then you need Cricut Access.

If you're not sure, you can always test it out by paying for the Perfect Starter plan.

Frequent Cricut Problems and Solutions

Now that you're familiar with Cricut models and the Cricut Design Space, there are some challenges that you might encounter while using your Cricut.

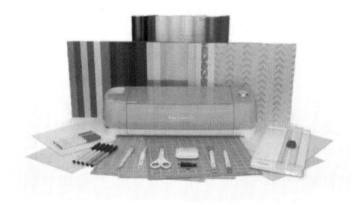

Photo credit: cricut.com

The problems that we will mention will also come with solutions that you can quickly put in place in your home.

Your Transfer Tape isn't working

Using a transfer tape can be complicated and difficult to use sometimes, but the most frustrating part of using it is when it is used on your project, but then, it doesn't come up.

This problem is usually common when working with glitter, vinyl, and even glitter vinyl. When your transfer tape seems not to be working, that's probably because you're using the wrong one.

Photo credit: persialou.com

Some rolls of vinyl, when purchased, come with their transfer tape, or they recommend one for you. But this isn't the same for every case.

For example, when working with some projects, the Standard transfer tape is ideal. This usually happens if you are making use of the standard vinyl.

But, for other types of vinyl, you should probably use the StrongGrip transfer tape made by Cricut.

If you're looking for something cheap and quick, you can use painter's tape or contact paper.

Your Material is Tearing

Different reasons cause this, but the main reason is probably because of your cutting mat. If your cutting mat isn't sticky enough, the material will keep on cutting.

There are many reasons why your mat might not be working right. It could be that you're using the wrong mat for your project or that the mat is old, and the stickiness has already weakened.

The blue Cricut mat is the Light Grip mat. This is good for materials that don't need a lot of stickiness to stay in a place, like paper.

Photo credit: cricut.com

The purple Cricut mat is the Strong Grip mat, which is ideal for those materials that slip around a lot and might get damaged. This includes leather and some types of fabric.

Then there's the green Cricut mat, which is the Standard Grip mat. It's for anything that's not too light and not too strong.

It's essential to use the right mat for your materials, or else, you'll waste a lot of your materials.

There are some other reasons why your materials might be tearing instead of cutting.

- The blade

Photo credit: help.cricut.com

Most often than not, you might have trouble with your blade. When using a blade, two things can go wrong. First, the blade might just be old and in need of replacement. Second, the blade you're using is not suitable for the material that you're cutting. We mentioned the deep cut and fine point blade in the earlier chapters.

It's better to use the fine point blade whenever possible, but when you need a heavy hand, you should use the deep cut blade. Try not to use the deep cut blade for a lot of materials, or they will tear.

- The settings

If none of the aforementioned works, you should also check the Design Space settings. You might not be using the right cut settings for the material.

Also, if the image that you're trying to cut out is very complicated, the material might cut it wrong because of the settings. So, you should change your cut settings to the cardstock intricate design settings.

- The type of material

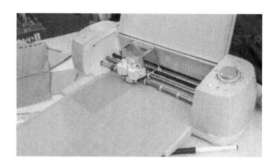

Photo credit: bestreviews.com

If nothing else works, then it might be safe to conclude that the material cannot be cut by your Cricut machine. There are over a hundred materials that can work with Cricut, and so this is highly unlikely.

But, if you've exhausted all your options, then you can test your machine with paper. If it cuts appropriately, you will know that the material you're trying to cut is not compatible with Cricut.

Your Blade isn't Cutting Right

If your blade isn't cutting right through the material, then that might cause problems for your design. There are a few solutions to this.

The most common mistake that people make is when they don't push their blade in all the way. If your blade isn't cutting through the material, ensure you placed the blade right.

Also, ensure that your blade is clean. If there is debris around your blade, then your blade won't work correctly. If there is debris, then you can clean the blade using compressed air.

Lastly, it could be your Cricut cut settings. Before cutting, you should check out the settings to make sure that everything is in place. If you want to clarify if the problem is the material, you can test the settings out with a small part of the material that you want to cut.

With these solutions, your blade should work right. If not, then your blade isn't right for the material that you're cutting.

Problems with Images

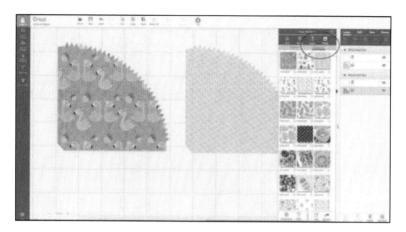

Photo credit: pinterest.com

- The images aren't showing on the mat

The first and common problem with images is when they aren't showing on the mat. This happens when you have made a perfect design on Cricut Design Space, but when you cut it, you don't see your images.

If you have this problem, it's straightforward to fix it. Go to your design, click on 'Group,' and then 'Attach' from the layers panel. This will ensure that your designs stay where you placed them, and so when you cut, everything will be where they're supposed to be.

- Converting images to SVG

Another problem is one of converting images to an SVG. SVG means Scalable Vector Graphics, and in Cricut, it is a file that is designed mathematically, and it is entirely compatible with Cricut. When you use an SVG file for your images, you will have no problem with the appearance of your pictures.

It's not always easy to find images that are already in SVG format, and so you will have to convert it to SVG using an online tool.

Luckily, many online tools convert PNG and JPG files to SVG, although not all of them work perfectly.

- Uploading images on Cricut

There is another problem of how to upload your designs and pictures. This is only possible with a Cricut Access Subscription. With this, you can use images that are not provided for you in Cricut Design Space.

Rest assured because you can always upload your images on your user-friendly Cricut Design Space.

Firstly, make sure that the picture you want to use does not need you to take permission before using it. It's safer to use pictures that you have rights to. When searching Google for images, you have to check out for the photos that you can use without asking for permission.

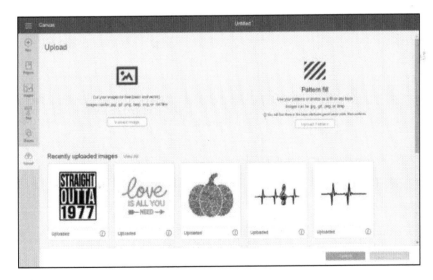

Photo credit: help.cricut.com

Also, the files have to be either .jpg, .png, .bmp, or .gif. These images can be edited while the uploading process is going on. If you don't find them, you can use .svg and .dxf files, although they are vectors. This means that as you upload, the layers will be separate.

Next, you open your canvas area to the design you want to add the image to or a blank page. Then you select if you're uploading an image or pattern fill. After that, choose if the image is complex, moderately complex, or simple.

Next, edit the picture so that it can flow with your design. Then, you click on continue; you will then choose if between 'print and cut' or just 'cut.'

If you think you will need your image again, you can save it to the application and use it at any time.

Your Cricut Design Space has stopped working

Every application, including Cricut Design Space, is prone to cashing, freezing or other challenges. There are some reasons why these problems can happen.

- Slow internet

This is the most common problem with Cricut Design Space refusing to work. Before you get angry at Cricut, you should check your internet connection.

For the Cricut Design Space to work efficiently, it needs consistent internet speed. This means that both in the area of uploading and downloading, your internet speed must be up to par for your Cricut program to work ideally. If not, you will experience problems like freezing.

If your internet connection is slow, you should place your device close to your modem. If this doesn't work, you should contact your service provider.

- The Browser

When using Cricut Design Space, your browser must be up to date to the latest version. You can use any browser when using Cricut. From Chrome and Mozilla to Firefox, any browser works as long as it's up to date.

If you're using a particular browser that is up to date and your Cricut Design Space isn't working, then you should switch to another browser. This usually works.

- Your device

The problem can also be on the phone, tablet, or computer that you're using. For Cricut Design Space, there are some specified minimum requirements that your computer must meet.

Apple Computers:

Your Mac computer must meet the following requirements.

- A CPU of 1.83 GHz.
- Free 50MB space.
- Have 4GB RAM.
- Must be Bluetooth capable and have a USB port.
- It must be the Mac OS X 10.12 or something more recent.

Photo credit: laptopswhizz.com

Windows Computers:

Your Windows computer must meet the following requirements.

- It must feature an Intel Core series or AMD processor.
- Free 50MB space or more.
- Have 4GB RAM.
- Must be Bluetooth capable and have a USB port.
- It must be Windows 8 or a newer version.

If your system meets these requirements and your Cricut Design Space isn't working still, then it could be because of Background Programs.

You could clear your cache and history, update your system, check for malware, or update your antivirus.

- Call Cricut Help Center

If all problems persist, then you call Cricut to fix the problem. The Design Space might be crashing or freezing because of an internal Cricut problem.

I hope that you're enjoying this book and learning a lot! If you are, I would love to see your opinion and review on Amazon!

CHAPTER FOUR

Maintaining Cricut

If you want your Cricut Machine to last for a very long time, you have to maintain it routinely. This means cleaning it properly and also maintaining the cutting mats and blades.

Maintaining the Cricut Machine

When using your Cricut machine, over time, it will inevitably collect paper particles, dust, and debris. Also, grease in the device will begin to stick to the carriage track.

Photo credit: youtube.com

If you want your machine to last long, then you should clean it regularly, or else it can get damaged prematurely. Here are some cleaning tips to help you out when cleaning the machine.

- Before cleaning your machine, disconnect it from the power outlet. This will prevent electrocution or any other accident that can damage the device or injure you.

- When cleaning your machine, don't use any form of acetone. Acetone, like nail polish remover, will damage the plastic parts of the device permanently.

- You can clean the machine using a glass cleaner instead. Spray it on a clean, soft cloth and wipe the device gently.

Photo credit: thewirecutter.com

- In the case of grease buildup on the carriage tracks, then you should use a tissue, cotton swab, or a soft, clean cloth to wipe it off gently.

- There is also the case of a buildup of static electricity on your machine. This can cause dust, debris, and particles to form on the device. This can also be easily cleaned with a soft, clean cloth.

Application of Grease for the Cricut Explore Models

- Disconnect the Cricut machine from the power outlet.

- Push the Cut Smart carriage gently to the left.

- Wipe the entire Cut Smart carriage bar with a tissue. The bar is the surface in front of the belt where the carriage slides on.

- Push the Cut Smart carriage gently to the right.

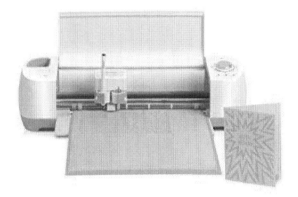

Photo credit: amazon.com

- Repeat the cleaning process for the other side by cleaning the bar with clean tissue.

- Then, push the Cut Smart carriage to the center of the bar.

- Take a lubrication packet, open it, and squeeze out a little grease. Put the amount of grease on a clean cotton swab.

- Apply a small coating of the grease on the two sides of the Cut Smart carriage around the bar so that it will form a quarter inches ring on both sides.

- In order to make the grease become even in the carriage, push the Cut Smart carriage to the both sides slowly and repeatedly.

- Clean off any grease that stained the bar while you were greasing the machine.

- You can purchase a grease packet from Cricut. This will work better than using a third-party grease packet so that the machine will not get damaged. This is especially if, after using another grease product, your Cricut machine is making a grinding sound.

- This process is almost the same as greasing your Cricut Maker machine too.

Maintaining the Cricut Cutting Mat

You also have to clean and maintain your Cricut cutting mat because that is where the cutting takes place.

If the cutting mat isn't clean, it can stain the machine. Also, if your cutting mat has stopped sticking, it can spoil your designs and creations.

When your mat is no longer sticky because of debris and grime, cleaning it and making it sticky again will bring it back to life.

The solutions that I will mention are not ideal for the pink cutting mats, only for the green, blue, and purple.

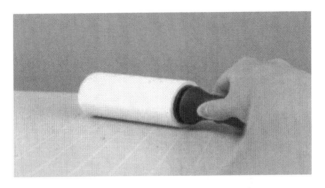

Photo credit: alittlecraftinyourday.com

There are many ways to clean your cutting mat.

- Using baby wipes:

Make use of alcohol-free, unscented, and bleach-free baby wipes to clean your mat. You should use the plainest baby wipes that you can find so that you don't add lotions, cornstarch, solvents or oils to your cutting mat. If not, you could affect the stickiness and adhesive of the mat. Also, after cleaning it, let it dry completely before using it.

- Using a Sticky Lint Roller

Photo credit: amazon.com

You can also use a roll of masking tape if you don't find a sticky lint roller. Run the roll across the mat to get rid of hairs, fibers, specks of dust, and paper particles.

This form of cleaning can be done daily or between projects so that dust doesn't accumulate on the mat. This is a fast way to remove dirt apart from using tweezers or scrapers.

- Using warm water with soap

You can also clean the mat with soap and warm water. You should use the plainest soap possible too so that you don't mess with the mat. Use a clean cloth, sponge, soft brush, or a magic eraser. Also, rinse it thoroughly and don't use it until it is completely dry.

- Using an adhesive remover

In the case of heavy-duty cleaning, then you should use a reliable adhesive remover to clean it properly. When using an adhesive remover, read the directions properly before you start.

Then, spray a little amount on the mat and spread it around with a scraper or anything that can act as a make-shift scraper.

Photo credit: alittlecraftinyourday.com

Wait for a few minutes so that the solvent can work on the mat. Then, scrape the dirty adhesive off your mat with a scraper, paper towels, or cloth.

After this, wash the mat with warm water and soap in case there is leftover residue and let it dry properly.

How to Make Your Cutting Mat Sticky Again

Photo credit: youtube.com

After washing or cleaning your cutting mat, you have to make them sticky again.

The most advisable way to make your mat sticky again is by adding glue to it. Get a solid glue stick like the Zig 2-Way Glue Pen and apply it on the inner portion of the mat. Then, stroke the glue around the mat and ensure that there is no glue residue on the edges of the mat.

After about 30 minutes, the glue will turn clear. If the cutting mat turns out to be too sticky after you apply glue, you can use a piece of fabric to reduce the adhesive by pressing the material on the parts of the mat that are very sticky.

Cover the mat with a clear film cover after a few hours.

You can also use tacky glues or spray adhesives that are ideal for cutting mats.

General Maintenance

- When your mat isn't in use, cover it with a clear film cover so that dust and hairs won't accumulate on the surface of the mat.

- Handle your mats with care. If you want to ensure that the adhesive does not get damaged, avoid touching the sticky surface with your hands.

Photo credit: inspiration.cricut.com

Always ensure that your mat dries entirely before using it or covering it up. Don't use heat when drying your mat, but you can place it in front of a fan. Also, ensure that it is drying hanging up so that both sides will dry.

Maintaining the Cricut Cutting Blade

You can use your Cricut fine point blade for over a year if you maintain it properly! The same goes for the other types of cutting blades. When maintaining your Cricut cutting blade, you have to keep it sharp all the time so that it does not get worn out.

Photo credit: brandpost.co.nz

Keeping your blade sharp is essential because if it isn't, it can damage your materials, and cause wastage. Also, if you don't maintain your blades, you will have to replace them often.

Keeping Your Cutting Blade Sharp

- Spread a portion of an aluminum foil on a cutting mat. Without removing the blade from the housing, cut out a simple design in the foil. This will sharpen the blade and remove any paper particles, or vinyl stuck on the blade. This can be used for any type of cutting blade.

- In the case of heavy-duty cleaning, you should squeeze a sheet of aluminum foil into a ball. You need to remove the blade from the housing of the machine to use this method. Then, depress the plunger, take the blade and stick it into the ball of aluminum foil repeatedly. You can do this 50 times. This will make it sharper and also remove vinyl or paper particles on the blade.

How to Store Your Cutting Blade

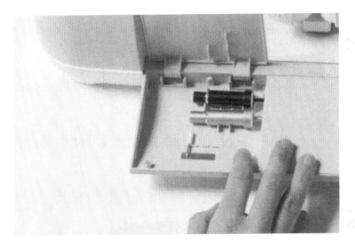

Photo credit: pinterest.com

The best way to store your cutting blade is to leave it in the Cricut compartment. You can place it in the drop-down door that is in front of the machine. That compartment is meant for storing the blade.

As for the blade housing, you can place it on the raised plastic points at the back of the machine. There are magnets in the front of the machine where you can stick loose blades.

When you put your blades in the Cricut machine, you never lose your blades.

CHAPTER FIVE

Cricut Model Comparison

From the first chapter, we introduced the four recent Cricut models that are available. They are the Cricut Explore One, Cricut Explore Air, Cricut Explore Air 2 and Cricut Maker.

With these choices, you might be wondering what the differences between them are and which one you should purchase.

I will explore these models briefly and later on, explain which Cricut machines you should use depending on how deep you are in the craft.

Cricut Explore One

Although this is the oldest contemporary Cricut machine and the oldest in the Explore line, it is still being purchased today because of its efficiency.

Photo credit: amazon.com

Explore One is ideal for beginners and inexperienced users who want to get into die-cutting, craft cutting, and plotting. The machine isn't advanced like the other Explore models, and it is also the cheapest Cricut machine you can get.

- Capability:

The machine is also highly capable, even if it's an old model. The system can also handle scoring and writing smoothly.

- Materials:

Photo credit: amazon.com

Regardless of the simplicity and the inexpensive nature of the machine, it is still highly capable. You can use this system to cut a range of 60 materials and more. This includes light materials like vinyl and thick materials like felt.

- Cutting Force

The machine comes with a topnotch German carbide premium blade, which can cut through thick and light materials alike neatly and cleanly. Even if Explore One is recommended for beginners, it is very professional. The blade is also highly durable.

As for the cutting width, the Explore One can cut sizes that range from 23 ½" tall and ¼ to 11 ½" wide.

Even though the Explore One seems excellent, there are some activities that you can't do on the Cricut Design Space if you're using this model.

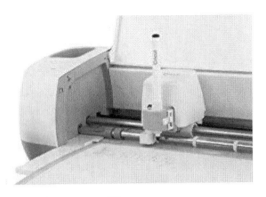

Photo credit: amazon.com

Cricut Design Space is very user friendly when using it for Explore One. It accepts .jpg, .png and .bmp files.

Also, the Cricut Explore One cannot function wirelessly. If you want to add convenience to it and you don't mind the cost, then you can buy a Bluetooth adapter and use it to transfer images or files wirelessly.

The Explore One also comes with one head clamp or carriage only. Because of this, if you want to draw and cut at the same time, you have to buy an adapter.

These are the tools that are in a newly purchased Explore One box:

- 24 x 9.5 x 9.5 sized Cricut Explore One machine.
- German carbide premium blade.
- Over 50 free images.
- Over 25 free one-click projects.
- 12" x 12" Standard Grip cutting mat.
- USB and power cords.

- Vinyl sample.
- Welcome guide.

Cricut Explore Air

Photo credit: amazon.com

While this is quite similar to the Explore One model, it also comes with some additional features. The main difference between them is the presence of the inbuilt Bluetooth adapter. If you don't enjoy seeing cables and wires all around your workplace, especially with the danger of tripping over them, then this model solves that problem.

- Capability

The Explore Air is also different from Explore One because it features a double carriage. This means that you can draw, write or score while you cut because it has two clamps to hold both tools. This saves you money because you don't have to purchase a tool adapter.

- Materials

The Explore Air is quite liberating when it comes to materials. It features a dial that can allow you to choose the material that you're about to cut. That way, you don't have to guess the blade depth and mess up the material.

The machine will know how deep it will have to cut for felt and how gentle it has to be for paper or vinyl. This feature is especially great for beginners who are not well versed with the blade depths.

For experienced users, the Cricut Explore Air also features several custom settings that allow the user to customize the cutting of their design.

This model can cut more materials than the Explore One, including fabric, poster board, vellum, and about 70 more.

- Cutting Force

Photo credit: businesswire.com

The system is more powerful than the older model when it comes to the cutting force. It features a Cut Smart technology made by Cricut, which enhances the blade control of the system and gives your creations a more professional look. It can cut anything that is as wide as 23.5 inches accurately and precisely.

It also has the Smart Set dial, which increases the control you have over the cutting of your project.

The features of the Cricut Design Space are very similar. But, when using Explore Air, you get more freedom, and you are allowed to use .svg, .gif, and .dxf files in addition to the standard files allowed with the Explore One.

Sadly, Explore Air does not have either a knife or a rotary blade. Because of these two types of blades, the Explore Air is recommended for more light crafts and scrapbooking. It does have an inbuilt blade, though.

A brand new Explore Air box comes with these tools:

- A 25.4 x 10 x 9.2 inches Cricut Explore Sir machine with inbuilt Bluetooth technology.
- It has an inbuilt accessory adapter.
- Inbuilt blade.
- USB and power cord.
- Metallic silver marker.
- Iron-on sample.
- Cardstock sample.
- Over 100 images,
- Over 50 ready-to-cut projects.
- 12" x 12" Standard Grip cutting mat.
- Welcome guide.

Cricut Explore Air 2

This is the youngest sibling of the Cricut Explore line. It is the best of the machines in this line. The Explore Air 2 is efficient like the other ones, but it does its work even better. It even has a better design, and it comes in different colors than you can do.

Photo credit: amazon.com

- Capability

The model features a Fast mode that speeds up the cutting process, primarily if you work with deadlines.

It also has the features in the other systems like the German carbide premium blade, inbuilt Bluetooth adapter, dual carriage, and auto-settings.

The great thing about the Explore Air is that it is ideal for both beginners and advanced users.

- Materials

This machine is able to cut through a hundred materials or even more. This includes and is not limited to cotton, silk, tissue paper, corkboard, foil, foam, aluminum, leather, clay, chipboard, burlap, and even birch wood.

It also has the Smart Dial, which helps you manage the cutting width depending on the materials.

- Cutting Force

Photo credit: cricut.com

The model is highly potent, and it makes use of the German carbide premium fine point blade, which comes with precision and speed. It is also able to cut any material with a width of 11.5 x 23.5 inches.

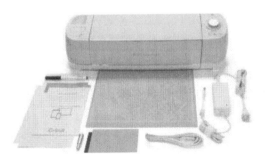

Photo credit: heatbusiness.com

When you first purchase a Cricut Explore Air 2, you get a three months free subscription with access to premium features offered by Cricut!

The Cricut Design Space is also cloud-based for those using iOS devices. With this, you can work offline!

The only downside in this model is the slightly increased noise level, but this is expected because it works two times faster than the previous models.

Your shiny, new Cricut Explore Air 2 will look like this:

- Cricut Explore Air 2 machine.
- Adapter.
- Power and USB cord.
- German carbide premium blade.
- Machine software and application.
- Built-in projects and images.
- Standard Grip cutting mat.
- Cardstock Sample.
- A pen.
- Welcome guide.

Cricut Maker

Photo credit: amazon.com

The newest Cricut die-cutting machine is the Cricut Maker. If you thought that the Explore Air 2 was a great model, then you should get ready to be blown away.

The Cricut Maker is a rare unit amongst other die-cutting machines. The rotary blade is already enough to attract experienced users. And, for beginners, it provides an avenue for improvement and unlimited creativity.

- Capability

The Cricut Maker, as an updated version of others, is very powerful and flexible. It comes with a toolkit that includes a rotary blade, knife blade, deep cut blade, and fine point blade. It also comes with a single and a double scoring wheel, as well as a collection of pens. The pens include a fine point pen, a washable fabric pen, a calligraphy pen, and a scoring stylus.

The machine also improves its efficiency by adding some unique features. We have the adaptive tool system, which means that the device can adjust the angle of the blade and the pressure of the blade automatically depending on the material. It doesn't need the Smart dial feature because the Cricut Maker determines your cutting force for you, and its decisions are usually accurate.

It has two clamps, one for the pen or scoring tool and the other for the cutting blade. This system is also unique because of its fast mode and precise mode. This works for any paper, cardstock, and vinyl.

- Materials

As expected, the Cricut Maker will be able to handle more and thicker materials than the machines in the Cricut Explore series.

From light materials to basswood and leather, this machine will exceed your expectations.

Cricut Design Space also provides a lot of benefits for Cricut Maker users/. It allows .jpg, .gif, .png, .svg, .bmp and .dxf files.

Photo credit: cricut.com

The system also supports wireless Bluetooth adapter. You can also enjoy the Sewing Pattern Library if you own a Cricut Maker. The library contains 50 ready-to-cut projects, and it is a result of a partnership between Cricut and Riley Blake Designs.

Another great benefit you get when using Cricut Maker with Design Space is that you get free membership of Cricut Access for a trial period.

Photo credit: heyletsmakestuff.com

The only downsides to this model are that it is quite slow when working with very thick materials, although that is expected. It also produces a lot of noise because of the fast mode.

This is what comes in the new Cricut Maker box.

- Cricut Maker machine.
- Rotary blade and drive housing.
- Fine point pen.
- Premium fine point pen and housing.
- USB cable.

- Power adapter.
- LightGrip Mat 12″ x 12″.
- FabricGrip Mat 12″ x 12″.
- Fifty ready-to-cut projects, which includes 25 sewing patterns.
- Materials for the first project.
- Welcome guide.

Which Cricut Model Should You Use?

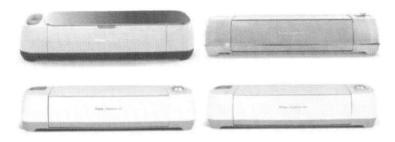

Photo credit: heyletsmakestuff.com

Although all Cricut models are great, the Cricut Maker or Explore Air models are highly recommended, whether you're a beginner or an advanced user. These two machines are usually ideal for most people, no matter the type of craft you use.

For the person who is looking to go into serious crafting, woodworking, sewing, and quilting, then the Cricut Maker is highly recommended. It is highly professional, and it can work for any craft that you're getting into. The system has a lot of benefits, especially on Design Space.

If you're a beginner who is looking to go deep into crafting, then you should also get the Cricut Maker because it will make no sense to purchase an old model, and then buy a new one when you have gained some experience.

You might be planning on using your Cricut machine for business purposes. This will mean that you will be repeating the same action occasionally. For this use, you can use the Cricut Explore Air 2 because it has a fast mode and many other advantages.

Beginners, leisurely crafters and those who have a tight budget will work better with the Cricut Explore One and Explore Air.

CHAPTER SIX

Frequently Asked Questions

Although we have answered, most of the questions that might come up when you start using your shiny, new Cricut machine, here are some questions that beginners usually have.

Photo credit: cricut.com

With these answers, you won't have any trouble when using your Cricut machine, and you can start running wild with your creativity!

Questions on Cricut Design Space

- *Can Cricut Design Space work on more than one mobile device or computer?*

Yes, it can! Cricut Design Space, as mentioned earlier, is cloud-based. No matter where you are or the kind of device that you are using, you can always use this application as long as it is compatible. If you're logged in at home, you can also log in on your phone if you're on the go.

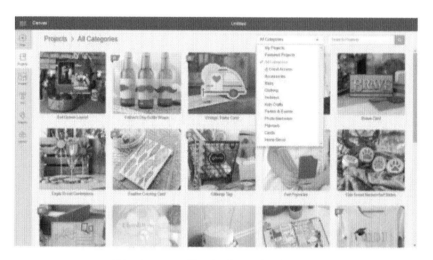

Photo credit: help.cricut.com

- *Do I have to have an internet connection before I use Cricut Design Space?*

Using Cricut Design Space on a laptop or a computer requires a high-speed internet connection. The internet must be high-speed broadband if you want your designing to go smoothly. iOS users can get the offline version of the app if they have the latest version of the Design Space.

- *Is there a difference between digital and physical cartridges?*

Photo credit: ithappensinablink.com

A cartridge, in the Cricut sense, generally refers to image sets. So, a cartridge is made up of images that have the same theme. Cartridges can be either digital or physical, although a lot of the physical cartridges have been re-tired. You can purchase the digital cartridges on cricut.com.

- *How do I find the Cricut Access fonts and images on Design Space?*

With their new update, everything that is available on Cricut Access has a green 'a' marking. This means that while you explore images and fonts, you can easily distinguish which one is from Cricut Access and which isn't. When searching for something, use filters too to narrow your search.

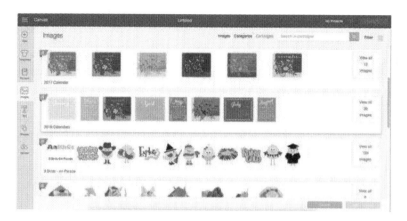

Photo credit: inspiration.cricut.com

- *How long do I own the images that I purchase on Design Space?*

Cricut images don't expire! That's right. Once you pay for them, you own them, and they remain in your library until you don't need them anymore.

- *Is it possible to disable the grid on the Canvas area?*

Yes, you can! If you're not comfortable or you don't want to use the gridlines, you can toggle them in your settings.

To do this, you open your Account menu and click on Settings. Click on Canvas Grid and from there, you can turn the grid lines off.

For those using an iOS device, Settings have been provided for you at the bottom of the screen. With them, you can turn the grid line on and off.

- *Is Design Space compatible with a Chromebook computer?*

No, it isn't. The latest version of Cricut Design Space only works with Windows or a Mac operating system.

Photo credit: inspiration.cricut.com

- *Do I need to pay in order to use Design Space?*

No, you don't. Design Space comes completely free. You only need a subscription if you plan on using Cricut Access. But, if you need the basics, then you can open a Design Space account for free.

Questions on all Cricut Machines

- *What is the Cricut tote bag?*

If you plan on travelling with your Cricut machine and supplies, or you need somewhere to store them when you're not using them, you can purchase a Cricut tote bag.

Photo credit: cricut.com

The Cricut machine tote bag is for all the cutting machines. It can fit anyone you own. The Cricut rolling craft tote bag is for supplies only, and the cutting machine can't fit in it. The kits come in Purple, Navy and Raspberry.

There is also the tweed Cricut tote bag which is an older version of the new tote bags.

- *Will my new Cricut Explore machine come with a carry bag?*

Photo credit: cricut.com

Sadly, it won't. This doesn't mean that you cannot buy a carry bag or machine tote back from Cricut separately.

- *Will a Cricut Maker fit into the tweed Machine Tote?*

Yes, it will. If you need somewhere to place your Cricut Maker for convenience, you can easily purchase a Machine Tote from Cricut.

- *Do I have to buy a Wireless Bluetooth Adapter when I buy an Explore machine?*

If you bought the Explore Air and Explore Air 2, you don't have to buy a Wireless Bluetooth Adapter. But this is not the same for the Explore One and so you can buy the Cricut Wireless Bluetooth Adapter if that's what you wish.

- *The Cricut Maker can know the blade I loaded without a Smart dial. How?*

The machine moves the carriage to the right before cutting your project. This is called homing. Here, the device will scan the blade and know which one you installed.

Photo credit: siserna.com

- *How do I download the software for Explore machines?*

To do this, first, go to design.cricut.com on your laptop or computer and log in with your Cricut ID. You will be guided through the process of downloading the Design Space plugin and installing it.

You can also use it on your phone by downloading the app from Google Play Store if you're an android user, or App Store if you're an iOS user.

- *If I upgrade from an Explore to a Cricut Maker, will I lose my projects and cartridges?*

No, you won't. All your information is not linked to the Cricut machine. Instead, it is connected to your Cricut ID in the Cricut Cloud. As long as you're using the same ID, you will have access to all your information and projects when you get a new Cricut machine.

- *Does my Cricut machine have to be connected to the internet?*

Your Cricut machine does not work alone but instead, it has to be connected to the Design Space. The Design Space uses an internet connection, except you're using the offline version on your iOS device.

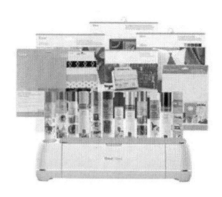

Photo credit: amazon.com

- *Do I use the same Design Space for both the Explore series and Cricut Maker?*

Your Design Space will definitely not change even if you are changing from one Cricut machine to another. Also, no matter which one you're using, you always have to use Design Space. But, Cricut Maker has more Design Space benefits than the Explore series.

CONCLUSION

Congratulations!

You are now well-versed in everything Cricut, and you're ready to take on your first project.

Photo credit: mix.com

If everything about Cricut and Cricut Design Space was overwhelming in the beginning, I'm sure that you're ready to start now.

Now, it's time to let your creative juices flow by starting on some simple projects.

Simple Projects to Start With

- Cricut Welcome Project.
- Paper flower corsages.
- Greeting cards.
- Paper decorations.
- Foam stamps.
- Personalized mugs, plates, candle jars and soap bottles.
- Doormat.
- Labels.
- Farmhouse signs.
- Personalized blankets and pillows.
- Felt projects like a garland.
- T-shirts, Socks, Totes and other fabrics.

Lucky for you, your Cricut machine will come with your first project for you to practice with, and if you get a Cricut Maker, you get materials for the project too.

After practicing, you can then try out some paper projects before moving on to vinyl and fabrics.

If you're interested in Cricut Access, you can also start with ready-to-cut projects so that you can learn how the cutting process works. If you're not ready to start designing, this is a good idea.

All in all, you will enjoy cutting simple projects with your new Cricut machine, and from there, you can move to the new ones.

Photo credit: cricut.com

General Tips for Beginners

- Start small:

You can't purchase a Cricut machine today and start cutting wood tomorrow. Even if you're planning on using your Cricut machine for the most complicated of projects, you should start small and use small projects to practice first.

- Get used to Design Space

Once you open your account on Design Space, use this guide to get conversant with all the panels and icons. Then, start with small and straightforward designs before you move to the more difficult and complicated ones.

- Constantly maintain the machine

Not just the device, but the accessories as well. If you want them to last for a very long time, then you have to handle them with care.

- Don't limit yourself

The great thing about Cricut is that it provides you with limitless opportunities and an excellent machine that helps you bring your designs to life. Don't limit yourself when you design with Cricut. Instead, go as far as your mind can take you.

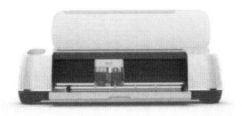

Your next creative leap starts here.

Whether you're new to crafting or an experienced maker, Cricut smart cutting machines and apps give you the freedom to make DIY magic happen anywhere, any day. Soon you'll be designing and cutting projects that wow even the pros.

Photo credit: cricut.com

You're Not a Beginner Anymore!

There you have it!

You now have everything you need to know at your fingertips. Study it all properly and start practicing now so that you can quickly get the hang of it.

If you've been looking at your Cricut machine collect dust, now is the time to pick it up; and if you've been considering purchasing one, now is the time to do so and let your creativity out!

If you were really helped by this book, feel free to let me know with a little review on Amazon!

CRICUT
PROJECT IDEAS

**Illustrated Guide To Create Many Unique Cricut Projects!
With Tips and Tricks for Beginners and Advanced for Cricut Design Space.**

Melissa Maker

Disclaimer

All erudition contained in this book is given for informational and educational purposes only. The author is not in any way accountable for any results or outcomes that emanate from using this material. Constructive attempts have been made to provide information that is both accurate and effective, but the author is not bound for the accuracy or use/misuse of this information.

INTRODUCTION

It is logical enough to assume that the abstract knowledge of Cricut has already been attained at this level. So much has previously been discussed on Cricut for beginners in the first version of this book. Nevertheless, let us do a swift recap of what Cricut is all about, just to be sure that we are on the same page all the way.

Photo credit- oleanschools.org

Cricut, as you have probably known, is basically a die-cutting machine. It gives you the ability to create something beautiful out of unique materials. It has been used by many to create such novelties as greeting cards, decorations, T-shirts, book covers, tote-bags, pop-up books, stickers, among many other things. In fact, new concepts are developed every now and then by creative people all over the world. Interestingly, many people still underutilize Cricut machines, being restricted to making a minute subset of what is possible, and I would not blame them too much for that. They are probably limited by their knowledge on how they can make use of it, not stylish enough, can't think creatively out of the box, or are just ignorant of the abilities of Cricut machines.

Now that you have already found your way to this book, it is time to stop using Cricut machines like a beginner and start using it professionally. This book will be giving a deep and better insight into how Cricut can be used ideally, and also how you can completely master every feature and function available in the machine and software. It will expose you to new vistas concerning the possibilities available to you, as a proud Cricut owner and user. To make you, the reader, understand every concept being discussed, many pictures and illustrations will be used. At the end of this book, I would like you to leave a positive review on Amazon if you benefit from every information shared here. Are you ready to become a professional and an active user of Cricut machines? Are you ready to get out of the box and let the creative juices flow freely? Brace yourself!

Models

To be very skillful, crafty, professional, and productive with your Cricut machine, you have to know your Cricut machine above all other things. There are various models of Cricut machines. Don't get confused; some Cricut machines may look the same according to design, functions, and features. However, no two of them are exactly the same. It doesn't matter if the same company produces them. So, let's go through these models and find out which one best serves your purpose.

Cricut Explore One

Photo credit- amazon.com

Although this model is quite old and has fewer features than the latest models, it is still one of the 'hottest' models ever produced. It is a die-cutting machine that has wireless capability (although the Bluetooth adapter has to be bought separately). It can cut through different unique materials such as paper, iron-on, fabric, adhesive vinyl, leather, and so on. It is known to be the only model with one tool slot among other models.

Cricut Explore Air

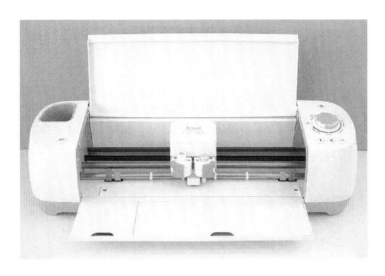

This Cricut machine is a wireless die-cutting machine that cuts through different materials like paper, faux leather, fabric, sticker paper, craft foam, vinyl, and so on. This model can also be utilized as a printer. Apart from its cutting abilities being slow and its outdated housing, it serves the same purpose as its next version.

Cricut Explore Air 2

There is just a minor upgrade between the first and second version of the Explore Air. With respect to speed and size, the Explore Air 2 serves a better purpose; it's small and two times faster than the previous version. Additionally, three new colors came with this version; Mint Blue, Giffin Lilac, and Rose Anna. The company labels this model as its DIY speed machine.

Cricut Maker

Photo credit- amazon.com

This model is designed for robustness and efficiency. Released in 2017, it cuts through thicker materials effortlessly and also comes with more tools. It is, up till date, known to be the ultimate smart die-cutting machine. More than 300 materials such as non-bonded fabric, basswood, felt, balsa wood, leather, etc., can be flawlessly cut through. It also comes with a rotary blade.

Accessories

Generally, almost all machines need specific accessories to function properly; the same goes for Cricut machines. There are some accessories you need to possess to use a Cricut machine effectively. Although the accessories you will need will be dependent on the nature of the project you want to work on, and how you want to work on it. There are several different accessories that work with Cricut machines; however, some are more important than others. Below are accessories you must have when using a Cricut machine, no matter what you are planning to create:

Cricut Cutting Mats

Photo credit- sursector.com

Cricut cutting mats are very important. They come in two different sizes; 12 X 12 and 12 X 24. They also have varying strengths. 12 X 12 mats are recommended if you have smaller materials; they come with a Light-grip mat, a Standard-grip mat, and a Strong-grip mat which are efficient enough for you to make different cuts on any material you want. You can also go for 12 X 24 if you need to work on longer materials. They also come with a Light-grip mat, a Standard-grip mat, and a Strong-grip mat. Light-grip mats are mostly used on lightweight materials like paper, vellum, or cardstock. Standard-grip mats are mostly used on medium-weight materials like vinyl, cardstock, iron-on, etc. If you have any material that has the tendency to slip a little while working on the mat, for example, heavy materials such as thick card stock or poster board, then make use of the Strong-grip mat.

Cricut Cutting Blades

Photo credit- help.cricut.com

Apparently, you can't cut without a blade. Therefore, the blade is one of the most necessary accessories you need to have. A typical Cricut machine should come with an ideal and effective blade. However, if you observe that your blades are not as sharp as they were, don't cut as clean as they used to, don't cut to your satisfaction, or you need an extra blade set, buy an original replacement blade, or trade your old or dull blade for a new one. There are two types of blades, depending on the machine model. We have the deep point blade and the bonded fabric blade.

The deep point blade is made of a durable and rigid steel. The blade angle is steeper, and it is recommended for materials such as chipboard, thick cardstock, magnet sheets, foam sheets, stamp material, cardboard, stiffened belt, and other related materials.

The bonded fabric blade looks exactly the same as the one that comes with Cricut machines. However, the housing and the blade itself are the more suited for fabric-grip mats. Since there are regular scissors and fabric scissors, it's only normal to have the regular blade (that comes with Cricut machines) and a fabric blade. Use the fabric blade to cut fabric materials only; it will retain its sharpness and cuts cleanly. Use the regular blade for other materials to balance it up.

Tools

Apart from the accessories discussed above, there are some other basic tools needed to run your Cricut machine smoothly and create designs. These tools range in function from facilitating use of the Cricut machine to trimming materials to easing difficulty of performing certain operations. Cricut has painstakingly created these tools to reduce the amount of effort required to take your idea from concept to reality. They include the following:

* Tweezers:

Photo credit- amazon.com.uk

Tweezers are perfect for holding and lifting small material pieces.

- Scissors:

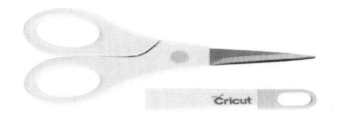

Photo credit- suzieqpapercrafts.com

Scissors are essential for cutting and resizing materials.

- Spatula:

Photo credit- suzieqpapercrafts.com

A spatula is also used to pick up cut pieces left on the mat. This relieves you of having to painstakingly use your hands to separate the cut material from the mat.

- Scraper:

Photo credit- amazon.com

This is used for weeding, which refers to scraping all left-overs scraps off cutting mats, a task that would ordinarily require use of your hands.

- Scoring Stylus:

Photo credit- michaels.com

This tool is used to insert fold lines when working on paper projects. It ensures that folds are proper and precise, and prevents errors, keeping your artworks neat.

- Paper Trimmer:

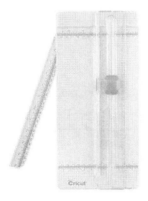

Photo credit- amazon.com

This is useful when working on materials with 12 X 12 size.

- Replacement Blade:

Photo credit- help.cricut.com

This extra blade will come in handy for trimming.

- Scoring Blade:

Photo credit- help.cricut.com

This is also used for trimming materials.

- Pens:

Photo credit- cricut.com

These are used to improve imperfect handwritings and designs.

- Cutting Ruler:

Photo credit- cricut.com

This is used to ensure perfect cutting line and to avoid rough edges.

- Rotary Cutter:

Photo credit- amazon.com

This tool is used to make perfect circle cuts. They come in handy for various designs which would otherwise be difficult to make using the regular cutters.

- Storage:

Photo credit- amazon.com

This small bag can be used to keep your working environment clean and tidy and also reduce the chances of losing a tool. It also allows you to organize your tools properly and increases their lifespan.

- BrightPad:

Photo credit- shopee.co.id

This is an amazing tool that allows users to see their work background. They can see every detail of their work while weeding, scuttling, tracing, or making pieces of jewelry. It is most effective on vinyl projects.

- CuttleBug:

Photo credit- personaldiecutting.com

This makes embossing look very easy and professional. You can comfortably modify papers, foils, leather, acetate, cardstock, and so on with this amazing tool.

- Aluminum Foil Ball:

Photo credit- overstock.com

This ensures that your blades are clean and sharp, thereby increasing their lifespan and effectiveness. The more you use it, the fewer reasons you have to buy replacement blades.

- Transfer Tape:

Photo credit- overstock.com

This is most especially useful for vinyl projects. It is used to transfer vinyl to the work surface. This will come in handy in heat transfer and iron-on projects especially when working with cloth.

- Cricut EasyPress:

Photo credit- orientaltrading.com

This makes iron-on projects easier to handle. It allows you to set the temperature and duration, reducing the likelihood of errors or damage to your designs or fabric.

There are so many other Cricut tools available to make Cricut projects easier, faster, more efficient, and more creative. To save money, you can go for the tool kit instead of single-tool purchases. Almost every tool you need are already packed inside the tool kit. To also go wireless and make designing more comfortable, you can buy a wireless Bluetooth adapter, especially if you are still using one of the old Cricut models. You can check these tools out in stores, both online and physical.

Materials To Use

There are hundreds of different materials that can be worked on with Cricut machines. To be precise, Cricut machines can cut through many materials that are precisely or below 2.0 millimeters thickness. Users with Circuit Maker models have more cutting force and size advantage. The Cricut Maker model cuts ten times faster and can put up with materials that are up to 2.4 millimeters thickness.

Photo credit- cricut.com

To be more organized, we will mention some of them by category. You may be familiar with some of them as a beginner. However, you can pick up new materials from these categories and start trying them out on new projects.

Paper and Cardstock: It seems somewhat necessary to start with this category because they are the most popularly used class of material when designing. They have over thirty-five different kinds of materials under them, therefore making them the category with the highest number of resources.

Vinyl: Professionals use vinyl materials a lot because they find it very effective and outstanding for making graphics, stencils, decals, signs, and so on. There are about 11 materials made from vinyl that can be used on Cricut machines.

Iron-On: This is also a vinyl product, but with different framework. Some people know it as heat transfer vinyl. You can make use of this type of vinyl to design and decorate tote bags, t-shirts, caps, and other clothing items. There are around 9 iron-on materials that are usable on Cricut machines.

Fabric and Textiles: Fabrics are naturals on Cricut machines; they work seamlessly on almost every Cricut machine model. There are about 17 different materials under this category. However, they, most of the time, need stabilizers to be added before cutting.

Infusible Ink: Infusible ink is an exciting material from Cricut which allows heat transfer on white and light-colored materials. It comes in different colors, patterns and gradients and is designed to be resistant to peeling, flaking and washing. It can be used for shirts, totes, coasters, etc.

Other Materials: Apart from all these five categories of materials we have discussed, there are several other unique materials that can be used on Cricut machines also. Ranging from by-products of foils, woods, sheets, board, Bellum, chips, tapes, to many other natural and artificial resources, there are at least 30 of them that can be worked upon by Cricut machines. There are materials people think are not compatible with Cricut machines. Well, you'd be surprised.

Cricut Maker: This also feels right to end with. It remains the first-rate and the most efficient Cricut machine ever produced. It has the capability to cut through more materials easily and steadily. The knife and rotary blade that come with it also puts it at an advantage over other Cricut machines when it comes to cutting materials. Over 125 fabrics can be used on the Cricut Maker model, and as mentioned before, it can handle materials that are 2.4 millimeters thick and below. Examples of materials that can be used on this model are; Velvet, Tweed, Tulle, Terry Cloth, Seersucker, Muslin, Moleskin, Knits, Jute, Jersey, Fleece, Cashmere, Chiffon, etc.

Now that a lot has been said about different types of materials that can be used on Cricut machines; you should be getting inspired to try out new different projects with these materials. However, only a beginner would stop here. We're not even close to unfolding the amazing parts of the usage of Cricut machines. You will get to know much later on in this book about the capabilities of Cricut machines and what you can do with them on an advanced level. Buckle up!

Where To Find Materials

One of the exciting parts of Cricut Design Space is that the materials are not hard to find; they are all around you. There are online stores where you can easily get the materials you want. Although different e-stores have varying prices, the point is to get the ideal quality.

There are four popular online stores where Cricut machine users, both beginners and professionals, get materials for their Cricut projects, and they are; Cricut.com, Amazon, Joann, and Michaels. These stores provide almost every supply and bundles you'll be needing. They have the materials, tools and accessories, and even the Cricut machines needed. Feel free to visit each store and compare their prices before purchasing.

Also, you can look around for stores in your local area where sell the most common types of materials that can be used on Cricut machines, mostly paper products.

At this stage, we have been able to cover most of the basics of Cricut machines, materials, tools and accessories. You should now know their functionalities and purposes to some extent. It's high time we proceeded to the technical and complex part of making use of Cricut for different designs and crafts. From here onward, we will not discuss much about the properties of Cricut machines, materials, tools, or accessories. It will be majorly about how you can set up your Cricut machine and what you can do with it. We're getting to the interesting parts.

However, before we get started, don't ignore the purpose of this introductory section. If you need to upgrade your Cricut machines, buy any material, tool or accessory, you should make plans for that now. The more resources you have, the more you can explore.

CHAPTER ONE

Setting Up The Machine

One way or another, you found yourself in possession of a Cricut machine and you have been worried about setting it up correctly? Well, there are lots of people like you on this table. Setting up your machine could look somehow complicated or tedious. However, this section is majorly written to guide you through it; the unboxing process and the setting up. So, relax and bring that Cricut machine out wherever you've stashed it. It takes approximately 1 hour to finish setting up a Cricut machine. With this guide, you should be done in less than an hour. Let's get right on it, shall we?

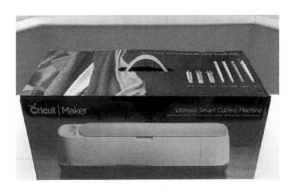

Photo credit- vinylcuttingmachines.net

STEP 1: OPENING THE BOX

To make sure that we are together all the way through, we will go through even the most trivial step; opening the box.

You should be having a number of boxes right now in front of you if you went for the whole Cricut bundle. And there should be a big box among those boxes which contains the Cricut machine itself. If you open that big box, the first thing you should find is a Welcome packet, most of the tools will be in that packet. You should find a welcome book, rotary blade and cover, a USB cable, a fine-point pen, a packet that contains your first die-cutting project. The USB cable is sometimes the last thing you'll see in this packet, it's hidden under every other stuff. Underneath this welcome packet is your Cricut machine.

To find the power cable, you first need to bring out the machine out from its box. You will then discover the power cable underneath the box with two cutting mats of standard sizes. That looked easy, right? Let's proceed to the next step.

Photo credit- daydreamintoreality.com

STEP 2: UNWRAPPING YOUR CRICUT MACHINE AND SUPPLIES

We are getting to the exciting part. Let's unwrap your machine and find out what's inside.

When trying to unwrap your machine, you'll find it covered in a protective wrapper that looks filmy and also with a cellophane layer. Try to carefully unwrap the top foam layer so you can see the machine clearly. After that, go on to remove the remaining part of the Styrofoam that protects the inner machine housing.

When you unbox the whole casing, you should expect to find the following tools;

- Cricut Machine
- USB and Power Cables
- Rotatory blade with housing.
- Fine point blade with housing
- Fine point pen.
- Light-Grip and Fabric-Grip Mats (12 x 12)

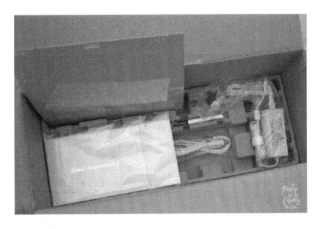

Photo credit- poofycheeks.com

STEP 3: SETTING UP YOUR MACHINE

Finally, we can move on to getting your machine up and running. Most of what you'll be doing will be technically inclined. You basically need electricity, a mobile phone or computer with internet access. Once you have access to all these, plug your power cord into an electronic outlet and then switch on your machine.

I'll assume your Cricut machine has Bluetooth function. If it does not have this function, either make use of the USB cable to connect your computer and the Cricut machine or purchase a Bluetooth adapter as soon as you can.

Photo credit- makezine.com

Once they are all connected, open your computer browser to continue the setup. Visit the **Cricut Sign-in Page** and click on the "Sign in" icon. You will have to either sign in with your account details or create a new account for yourself if you don't already have one. This is necessary so as to be able to access the Cricut Design Space.

Photo credit- help.cricut.com

If you do not have an active account yet, don't bother to fill any information on the sign-in fields. Click on the "Create Cricut ID" in the green box and then fill out every field with the required information and click on "Submit."

Photo credit- cricut.com

Now, it's time to link your machine to your account. It takes some people a lot of time to finish this part successfully. To make it easier, follow the procedures below.

- After signing in, go to the upper left corner of the page and click on the drop-down menu icon (with three lines) beside "Home."

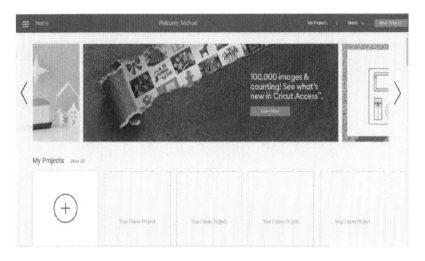

Photo credit- cricut.com

When the drop-down menu appears, select the "New Machine Setup."

- On the next screen that pops up, click on your Cricut machine model.

Photo credit- cricut.com

- Another webpage will appear with instructions on how to connect your machine. Follow the instruction accordingly.

When you follow the instructions, it automatically detects your machine and prompts you to download and install the software.

The site is user-friendly, so you'll be directed on how to go about the installation. And if you already have an account, you may still need to download it again. Cricut updates their design space often, there could be some new tools in the latest version that you don't have access to. It only takes about five minutes to get the installation done.

And there we go; we have concluded the setup procedure on your PC. That wasn't too hard, was it?

You might find the software a little bit complex for you when you first start to explore it. But with constant usage, you'll master it.

STEP 4: CLAIMING YOUR BONUS

When you have successfully created an active account on Cricut, you can claim access to Cricut for a whole month for free! It's a welcome bonus from Cricut. You'll have access to different projects, fonts, as well as Cut files. You can exploit this opportunity by making use of the accessible library to work on several fun projects.

STEP 5: COMMENCING YOUR FIRST PROJECT

You may want to start practicing with some old projects done by other people or study how they are done before you initiate your personal project. Every Cricut machine comes with a trivial project. You'll find it in the welcome pack. You can use this to get familiar with the tools the machine came with.

Photo credit- cricut.com

It may be a little bit difficult to make use of the Cricut Design Space without fully knowing its environment. So, stick with small projects till you get better, or ask someone who has more knowledge and experience with Cricut tools to guide you through. You should have enough proficiency with these tools before moving to the next chapter. The next chapter will be discussing projects on a professional level. Ready when you are...

CHAPTER TWO

Project Ideas By Craft

People use Cricut for so many reasons. Some for business purpose and some for their personal reasons. However, there are so many projects you can work on irrespective of your purpose. I will be mentioning a FEW of the projects you can make with your Cricut machine. Feel free to challenge yourself with any of them when you have the resources. They are categorized according to their crafts. The level of difficulty of these project ideas varies, it all depends on how skillful you are with the Cricut Design Space and the machine itself.

Paper Crafts

1. Bookmarks
2. Cake Toppers
3. Cards
4. Crepe Paper Flowers
5. Cupcake Toppers
6. Die Cuts
7. Embroidery Hoop Wreath
8. Fairy Houses
9. Favor Boxes
10. Geometric Wall Art
11. Giant Paper Flowers (Nursery Decoration, Free Standing Paper Flower, K-drops, etc.)
12. Gift Tags

13. Packaging Stickers (Labels, Thank-you Stickers, etc.)
14. Paper Botanicals
15. Paper Bows
16. Paper Crowns
17. Paper Dresses
18. Paper Fans
19. Paper Flower Crowns
20. Paper Garland
21. Paper Houses
22. Paper Lanterns
23. Paper Leis
24. Paper Ornaments
25. Paper Scenes
26. Paper Straws
27. Party Banners
28. Party Hats
29. Planner Stickers
30. Princess Centerpieces
31. Shadow Boxes with Paper Crafts
32. Small Paper Flowers (Arrangements, Corsages, Wreathes, Paper flower bouquets, etc.)

Adhesive Vinyl Crafts

1. Birth Stats Board
2. Computer Decals
3. Cookies-for-Santa plates
4. Cricut Machine Decals
5. Custom Balloons
6. Custom Cake Stands
7. Custom Mugs
8. Custom Piggy Banks
9. Dog Bowls
10. Dog Treat Jar
11. Door Mats

12. Food Tray
13. Front Door Decals
14. Growth Chart
15. Hand-Lettered Sign
16. Hot Mess Canvas Art
17. Jewelry Dishes
18. Kitchen Crock Pot
19. Kitchen Labels
20. License Plates
21. Makeup Brush Holders
22. Mason Jars
23. Menu Board or Calendar
24. Mixer Decals
25. Monogram Notebooks
26. Monogram Plates
27. Ornaments
28. Phone Cases
29. Planters
30. Stove Cover
31. Tumblers
32. Vinyl Clipboards
33. Water Bottles
34. Wood Signs

Iron-On Vinyl Crafts

1. Aprons
2. Baby Onesies
3. Bath Towels
4. Beer Cozies
5. Blankets
6. Canvas Shoes
7. Custom Socks
8. Cutting Boards
9. Drawstring Bags
10. Garden Signs

11. Hats
12. Hot Pads
13. Make-up Bag
14. Pillows
15. Tea Towels
16. Tote Bags
17. T-shirts
18. Wood Hangers

Wood Crafts

1. Bunting Banner
2. Burp Clothes
3. Cake Topper
4. Coasters
5. Cosmetic Bag
6. Doll Clothes
7. Dolls and Soft Toys
8. Earrings

Fabric Crafts

1. Family Tree
2. Felt Flowers
3. Hair bows
4. Key Chains
5. Kids Alphabet Letters
6. Leather Earrings
7. Leather Journal Cover
8. Leather Wallet
9. Quilts
10. Script Sign
11. Sleep Masks
12. Tassel Garland
13. Wood Letters for Signs

14. Wood Ornaments

Like I mentioned earlier, these are just a FEW of the hundreds of projects you can make with your Cricut machines. There are still many project ideas out there. Moreover, you can be creative enough to design a project by inspiration. Some people created these projects, and there's nothing stopping you from inventing new crafts. The only limits exist, literally, in your mind.

CHAPTER THREE

Step-By-Step Guide on Some Cricut Projects

Now that you have learnt how to set up and use your Cricut machine, it is time to actually use it to bring those fantastic projects you have always dreamed about to life. In this chapter, we will create a few projects using the different tools and materials that you have learnt about so far. We have tried to include projects diverse enough to provide an exhaustive view of the capabilities of your Cricut machine and to give you a good idea of what possibilities exist in expressing your yet untapped creativity and undiscovered potential.

Felt Roses

MATERIALS NEEDED:

SVG files with 3D flower design

Felt Sheets

Fabric Grip Mat

Glue Gun

Photo credit- printablecrush.com

STEPS:

- First of all, upload your Flower SVG Graphics into the Cricut design space as explained in the "Tips" section. ("How to import images into Cricut Design Space)
- Having placed the image in the project, select it, right-click and click "Ungroup". This allows you to resize each flower independent of the others. Since you are using felt, it is recommended that each of the flowers are at least 6 inches in size.

- Create several copies of the flowers, as many as you wish, selecting the colors you want in the Color Sync Panel (by dragging and dropping the images on to the color you would want them to be cut on). Immediately you're through with that, click on "Make it" on the Cricut design space.
- Click on "Continue". After your Cricut Maker is connected and registered, under the "materials" options, select "Felt".
- If your *rotary blade* is not in the machine, insert it. Next, on the Fabric Grip Mat, place the first felt sheet (in order of color), then, load them into your Cricut Maker. Press the "cut" button when this is done.
- After they are cut, begin to roll the cut flowers one by one. Do this from the outside in. Make sure that you do not roll them too tight. Use the picture as a guide.
- Apply Hot Glue on the circle right in the middle and press the felt flowers that you rolled up on the glue. Hold this in place and do not let it go until the glue binds it.
- Wait for the glue to dry, and your roses are ready for use.

Custom Coasters

MATERIALS NEEDED:

Free Pattern Templates

Monogram Design (in Design Space)

Cardstock or Printing Paper

Butcher Paper

Lint-free towel

Round Coaster Blanks

LightGrip Mat

EasyPress 2 (6" x 7" recommended)

EasyPress Mat

Infusible Ink Pens

Heat Resistant Tape

Cricut BrightPad (optional) for easier tracing)

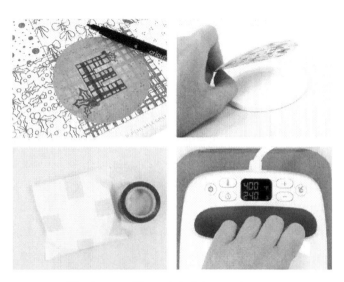

Photo credit- printablecrush.com

STEPS:

- In Cricut Design Space, open the monogram design. You can click "Customize" and choose the designs that you want to cut out or just go ahead and cut out all the letters.
- Click on "Make It".
- On the page displayed, click on "Mirror Image" to make the image mirrored. This must be done whenever you are using infusible ink. For your material, choose "Cardstock". Then, place your cardstock on the mat and load it into the machine; then press the "Cut" button on the Cricut machine.
- After the Cricut machine is done cutting, unload it and remove the done monograms from the mat.
- Trace the designs onto the cut-out. If you have a Cricut BrightPad, you can use it to carry out this step much more easily, as it will make the trace lines easier to identify. Tracing should be done using Cricut Infusible Ink Pens.

- Use the lint-free towel to wipe the coaster. Ensure that no residue is left behind to prevent any marks being left on the blank.
- Make the design centered on the face down coaster.
- Get a piece of butcher paper which is about an inch larger on each side of the coaster and place on top of the design.
- Tape this butcher paper onto the coaster using heat resistant tape, to hold the design fast.
- Set the temperature of your EasyPress to 400 degrees and set the timer to 240 seconds.
- Place another butcher paper piece on your EasyPress mat, set the coaster on top of it, face up.
- Place another piece of butcher paper on top of these. Place the already preheated EasyPress on top of the coaster, and start the timer.
- Lightly hold the EasyPress in place (without moving) or leave it in place right on the coaster – if on a perfectly flat surface – till the timer goes off.
- After this is done, gently remove the EasyPress 2 then turn it off.
- The coaster will be very hot, so you should leave it to get cool before you touch it. When it is cool, you can peel the design off of it.

Customized Doormat

MATERIALS NEEDED:

Cricut Machine

Scrap cardstock (The color does not matter)

Coir mat (18" x 30")

Outdoor acrylic paint

Vinyl stencil

Transfer tape

Flat round paintbrush

Cutting mat (12" x 24")

Photo credit- youtube.com

STEPS:

- Create your design in Cricut Design Space. You can also download an SVG design of your choice and import into Cricut Design Space. Make sure that your design is the right size; resize it to ensure that this is so.
- Next, you are to cut the stencil. You do this by clicking "Make it" in Cricut Design Space when you are done with the design. After this, you select "Cardstock" as the material. Then, you press the "Cut" button on the Cricut machine.
- When this is done, remove the stencil from the machine and weed.
- Next, on the reverse side of the stencil, apply spray glue. After this, attach the stencil to the doormat, exactly where you want your design to be; then, pick up the letter bits left on the cutting mat and glue them to their places in the stencil on the doormat.
- The next step is to mask the parts of the doormat which you do not want to paint on. You can do this using painters' plastic.
- Now, it's time to spray-paint your stencil on the doormat. Keeping the paint can about 5 inches away from the doormat, spray up and down, keeping the can pointed straight through the stencil. If it is at an angle, the paint will get under the stencil and ruin your design. Spray the entire stencil 2-3 times to make sure that you do not miss any part and that the paint is even.
- You're just about done! Now, remove the masking plastic and the stencil and leave the doormat for about one hour to get dry.

T-Shirts (Vinyl, Iron On)

To make custom t-shirts using your Cricut machine, you will need to use iron-on or heat transfer vinyl. Ensure that you choose a color that contrasts and matches well with your t-shirt.

MATERIALS NEEDED:

Cricut Machine

T-shirt

Iron on or heat transfer vinyl

Fine point blade and light grip mat

Weeding tools

EasyPress (regular household iron works fine too, with a little extra work)

Small towel and Parchment paper

STEPS:

- In preparing for this project, Cricut recommends that you prewash the cloth without using any fabric softener before applying the iron-on or heat transfer vinyl on it. Ensure that your T-shirt is dry and ready before you proceed.
- On Cricut Design Space, create your design or import your SVG as described in the section on importing images.
- If you are using an SVG file, select it and click on "Insert Images". When you do this, the image will appear in the Design Space canvas area.
- Then, you need to resize the image to fit the T-shirt. To do this, select all the elements, then set the height and width in the edit panel area, or simply drag the handle on the lower right corner of the selection.
- After this is done, select all the layers and click "Attach" at the bottom of the "Layers" panel, so that the

machine cuts everything just as it is displayed on the canvas area.

- You can preview your design using Design Space's templates. You access this by clicking the icon called "templates" on the left panel of Design Space's canvas. There, you can choose what surface on which to visualize your design. Choose the color of your vinyl and of the T-shirt so you can see how it will look once completed.

- Once you are satisfied with the appearance of your design, click "Make It". If you have not connected your machine, you will be prompted to do so.

- When the "Prepare" page shows, there is a "Mirror" option on the left panel. Ensure that you turn this on. This will make the machine cut it in reverse, as the top is the part that goes on to the T-shirt. Click "Continue".

- Next, you are to select the material. When using the Cricut Maker, you will do this in Cricut Design Space. Choose "Everyday Iron-On". On Cricut Explore Air, you select the material using the smart set dial *on the machine*. Set this dial to "Iron-On".

- Now, it's time to cut. To cut vinyl (and other such light materials), you should use the light-grip blue mat. Place the iron-on vinyl on the mat with the dull side facing up. Ensure that there are no bubbles on the vinyl; you can do this using the scraper.

- Install the fine point blade in the Cricut machine, then load the mat with the vinyl on it by tapping the small arrow on the machine. Then, press the "make it" button. When the machine is done cutting the vinyl, Cricut Design Space will notify you. When this happens, unload the mat.

- With the cutting done, it is time to weed. This must be done patiently, so that you don not cut out the wrong parts. Therefore, you should have the design open as a guide.

- After weeding, it is finally time to transfer the vinyl to the T-shirt. Before this, ensure that you have pre-washed the T-shirt without fabric softener, as mentioned at the beginning of this project.
- To transfer the design, you can use the EasyPress or a regular pressing iron. Using a pressing iron may be a little more difficult, but it is certainly doable. Before you transfer, ensure that you have the EasyPress mat or a towel behind the material on to which you want to transfer the design so as to allow the material to be pressed harder against the heat.
- Set the EasyPress to the temperature recommended on the Cricut heat guide for your chosen heat-transfer material and base material. For a combination of iron-on vinyl and cotton, the temperature should be set to 330ºF. After preheating the EasyPress, get rid of wrinkles on the T-shirt and press the EasyPress on it for about 5 seconds. Then, place the design on the T-shirt and apply pressure for 30 seconds. After this, apply the EasyPress on the back of the T-shirt for about 15 seconds.
- If you're using a pressing iron, the process is similar; only that you need to preheat the iron to max heat and place a thin cloth on the design, such that the iron does not have direct contact with the design or the T-shirt. This will prevent you from burning the T-shirt.
- Wait for the design to cool off a bit, then peel it off while it is still a little warm.
- Ensure that you wait for at least 24 hours after this before washing the T-shirt. When you do wash it, be sure to dry it inside out. Also, do not bleach the T-shirt.

3d Paper Flowers (Paper)

MATERIALS NEEDED:

Cricut Machine

Cricut mat

Colored scrapbook paper

Hot glue gun and glue sticks

Photo credit- pininterest.com

STEPS:

- To make flowers, you need an appropriate shape for the petals. To make such a shape, you can combine three ovals of equal size. To create an oval, select the circle tool, then create a circle. Then click the unlock button at the bottom of the shape. Once this is done, you can reshape the circle to form an oval.
- Duplicate this oval twice and rotate each duplicate a little, keeping the bottom at the same point, as shown in the picture.

- Select all three ovals and weld them together to get your custom petal shape. For each large flower, you need 12 petals – each one about 3 inches long, while for each small flower, you need 8 petals – each one about 2 inches long. For each flower, you also need a circle shape for the base of about the same width as each petal. Arrange the petals and base circle shape in Cricut Design Studio.
- Set your material to cardstock on Design Space or on the machine, depending on your machine, then cut the petals out.
- After you cut out the petals, remove them and cut a slit about half an inch long in the bottom of each one. Place a bit of glue on the left side and glue the right side over the glue for each petal.
- The next thing to do is to place the petals on the circle base. For large flowers, you need three circles of four petals each. For small flowers, you need five circles on the outside and three on the inside. Put a bit of hot glue on the petal and add to the circle as described above.
- For the center of the flowers, search Cricut Access for "flower" and chose shapes with several small petals. Cut these out using a different color of cardstock and glue to the center of the flowers.

Luminaries

MATERIALS NEEDED:

Luminary Graphic (From a Cricut Project)

Sugar Skull (SVG File)

Cricut Explore Air or Cricut Maker

Cardstock Sampler

Scoring Stylus

Glue Stick

Battery-Operated Tea Light

Photo credit- printablecrush.com

STEPS:

- The first step is to open your Luminary graphic on the Design Space.

- Then go ahead to upload the SVG file of your Sugar Skull and adjust its size to around 3.25" high. After doing that, move the Sugar Skull to the bigger part of the Luminary graphic (in the middle of the two score lines) and center-align it.
- Select the Sugar Skull and the Luminary Graphic and then go ahead and click on "Weld".
- Try selecting every graphic on the design space and click on "Attach." Then copy and paste the selected graphics on the same page (duplication).
- Select "Make It" at the topmost right-hand corner, and then ensure everything is positioned correctly. Click on "Continue." If you notice the files being cut on two different mats, just move them back together on one single mat by simply clicking on these three dots located at the graphic corner.
- Select "Light Cardstock" under the "Materials" menu, and then start loading the Mat and Cut. Also ensure that your Scoring Stylus is in Clamp A. This will automatically change your machine settings from scoring to cutting.
- When the cut-out is done, fold it along the Score lines. Then start gluing the small Flap to the interior part of the lantern's back.
- Switch on the Battery-Operated Tea Light, and then place your lantern on top of it.

Shamrock Earrings

MATERIALS NEEDED:

Cricut Maker

Earring (from a Cricut Project)

Rotary Wheel

Knife Blade

FabricGrip Mat

StrongGrip Mat

Weeder Tool

Cricut Leather

Scraper Tool

Adhesive

Pebbled-Faux Leather

Earring Hooks

Photo credit- printablecrush.com

STEPS:

- First, open the Cricut Project (Earring). You can now either click on "Make It" or "Customize" to edit it.
- Once you've selected one, click on "Continue."
- Immediately the Cut page pops up, select your material and wait for the "Load" tools and Mat to appear.
- Make your Knife blade your cutting tool in clamp B. This will be used on the Leather.
- On the StrongGrip Mat, place the Leather and make sure it's facing down. Then load the Mat into the machine and tap the "Cut" flashing button.
- When the scoring has been done, go back to the cutting tool and change it to Rotary Wheel so that you can use it on the Faux Leather.
- Similarly, place your Faux leather on your FabricGrip Mat, facing down. Then load the Mat into the machine and tap the "Cut" flashing button.
- Take away all the items on the Mat with your Scraper tool. Be careful with the small fringes though.
- Make a hole on the top circle by making use of the Weeder tool. Make sure the hole is large enough to make the Earring hooks fit in.
- If necessary, you may have to twist the hook's end with the pliers to fit them in.

- Close them up after you have looped it inside the hole that was made inside the Earring.
- Finally, you should glue the Shamrock to the surface of the Earring with adhesive. Wait for it to dry before using.

Valentine's Day Classroom Cards

MATERIALS NEEDED:

Cricut Maker

Card Designs (Write Stuff Coloring)

Cricut Design Space

Dual Scoring Wheel

Pens

Cardstock

Crayons

Shimmer Paper

Photo credit- printablecrush.com

STEPS:

- Open the Card Designs (Write Stuff Coloring) on the Design Space, and then click on "Make it" or "Customize" to make edits.

- When all the changes have been done, Cricut will request you to select a material. Select Cardstock for the Cards and Shimmer Paper for the Envelopes.
- Cricut will send you a notification when you need to change the pen colors while creating the Card, and then it will start carving the Card out automatically.
- You will be prompted later on to change the blade because of the Double Scoring Wheel. It is advisable to use the Double Scoring Wheel with Shimmer Paper; they both work best together.
- When the scoring has been finished, replace the Scoring Wheel with the previous blade.
- After that, fold the flaps at the Score lines in the direction of the paper's white side, and then attach the Side Tabs to the exterior of the Bottom Tab by gluing them together.
- You may now write "From:" and "To:" before placing the Crayons into the Slots.
- Place the Cards inside the Envelopes and tag it with a sharp object.

Glitter And Felt Hair Bow Supplies

MATERIALS NEEDED:

Hair bow project file in Cricut Design Space

Cricut Felt

Glitter Iron-on Vinyl

Hair Clips (large and small)

Cricut Mat

Glue Gun

Scissors and Weeding tools

EasyPress

Photo credit- printablecrush.com

STEPS:

- To start, in Cricut Design Space, open the design (hair bow); then, click "Make it now". If you would like to make any modifications to the design, click "Customize".

- Insert a regular blade into the Cricut machine. Then place the materials and the appropriate board on the Cricut mat.
- Send the document to the Cricut machine and cut it out.
- After the Cricut machine has cut out the felt and the iron-on, proceed to remove the excess vinyl, then cut around each of the bows using scissors.
- Heat up your EasyPress. For the appropriate settings, check the EasyPress Guide.
- Place the vinyl on the cut out felt, sticky side down, then heat with the EasyPress for 10 seconds. For larger pieces, do this for each section one at a time, after which you should smooth the EasyPress over the entire design.
- Remove the transfer paper and repeat this for all the other bows.
- Use the glue to stick one side of the bigger bow piece (the piece without the sharp edges) to the other side. This will form a circle.
- Apply glue on the inside and on the middle of that bow piece. After this, fold the piece so that it forms a bow.
- Stick the bow to its back piece.
- Fold the small bow piece to the middle of the bow. Fold it in the back and glue it also.
- Glue the bow to the bigger or smaller bow clips to have your bow.

Halloween T-Shirt

MATERIALS NEEDED:

T-shirt Blanks

Glam Halloween SVG Files

Cardstock

Transfer Sheets (Black and Pink)

Butcher Paper (comes with Infusible Ink rolls)

LightGrip Mat

EasyPress (12" x 10" size recommended)

EasyPress Mat

Lint Roller

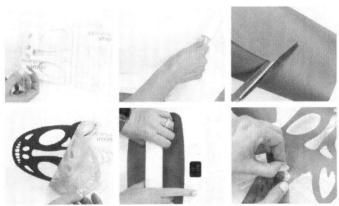

Photo credit- printablecrush.com

STEPS:

- Import the SVG files into Cricut Design Space and arrange them as you want them on the T-shirt.

- Change the sizes of the designs so as to get them to fit on the T-shirt.
- Using the slice tool, slice the pink band away from the hat's bowler part (the largest piece). Make a copy of this band, and then slice it from the lower part of the hat. With these done, you with have three pieces that fit together.
- You can change the designs' colors as you would like them. When you are done with the preparation, click "Make It".
- Ensure that you invert your image using the "Mirror" toggle. This is even more important if there is text on your design, as infusible ink designs should be done in inverse. This is because the part with the ink is to go right on the destination material.
- Click on "Continue"
- For the material. Select Infusible ink. After this, cut the design out using your Cricut Machine.
- With the designs cut out, weed the transfer sheet.
- Cut around the designs such that the transfer tape does not cover any part of the infusible ink sheet. Make sure that this is done well as any part of the infusible ink that is not in contact with the fabric will not be transferred.
- Preheat your EasyPress to 385 degrees, and set your EasyPress mat.
- Prepare your T-shirt by placing it on the EasyPress mat, then using a lint roller to remove any lint from the front.
- Insert the Cardstock in the t-shirt, between the front and back, just where the design will be. This will protect the other side of the T-shirt from having the Infusible Ink on it.
- If necessary, use the lint roller on the T-shirt again, after which you should heat your shirt with the Easy-Press. Do this at 385 degrees for 15 seconds.

- Turn the part where the design faces on the T-shirt. Place the butcher paper on the design, ensuring, again, that the backing does not overlap the design.
- Place the EasyPress over the design, and hold it in place for 40 seconds. Do not move the EasyPress around so that your design does not end up looking smudged.
- Remove the EasyPress from the shirt and remove the transfer sheet.
- To layer colors, ensure that your cutting around the transfer sheet is done as close as possible, then repeat the previous three steps for each color. This will prevent the transfer sheet from removing part of the color on the previously transferred design.

Hand Lettered Cake Topper

MATERIALS NEEDED:

Glitter Card Stock

Gold Paper Straw

Cutting Mat

Hot Glue Gun

Photo credit- printablecrush.com

STEPS:

- Create your design in Cricut Design Space, or download your desired design and import it into Cricut Design Space using the instructions in the "Tips" section.
- Resize the design as required.
- Click the "Make it" button.
- Select Glitter card stock as your material in Design Space and set the dial on your Cricut machine to "Custom".
- Place the glitter card stock on your Cutting Mat and load it into the Cricut machine.
- When this is done, press the "Cut" button on your Cricut machine.
- After the machine is done with cutting the design, remove it from the mat. This can be done much more quickly using the Cricut Spatula tool.
- Finally, using hot glue, stick cut out design to the Gold Paper Straw and stick it in the cake as shown in the picture.

Unicorn Free Printable

MATERIALS NEEDED:

Printables

White Card Stock

Cricut Mat

Crepe Paper Streamers (varied colors)

Gold Straws

Glue Stick

Hot Glue Gun

Scissors

Photo credit- printablecrush.com

STEPS:

- Import the printable image into Cricut Design Space, following the instructions under the "Tips" section of this book.
- Resize the PNG image and make it 5" wide.

- With your Cricut machine, cut the unicorn head using the white cardstock. Also, print and cut out the "stickers."
- After cutting out the pieces, stick the horn and the other elements using the glue stick.
- In each color, cut out strips of crepe paper, about 2" wide; then, cut each strip into thirds.
- On the reverse side of the unicorn head, glue the strips on the back edge (of the head), then glue on the top by the horn. Ensure that only half the length of each strip is on this side, as you are going to glue the other half on the other side of the unicorn head.
- Turn the unicorn head back over and glue the crepe streamers in place.
- Turn the head over yet again and use hot glue to stick the gold paper straw onto the unicorn head reverse side to use as party props.

Custom Back To School Supplies

This tutorial will show you how to use your iPad to create and convert designs for your Cricut machine to cut!

MATERIALS NEEDED:

Vinyl

Standard Grip Mat

White Paper

Markers (including black)

Pencil Case

3 Ring Binder

IPad Pro (optional)

Apple Pencil

Cricut Design Space App

Drawing app (e.g. ProCreate)

ProCreate Brushes

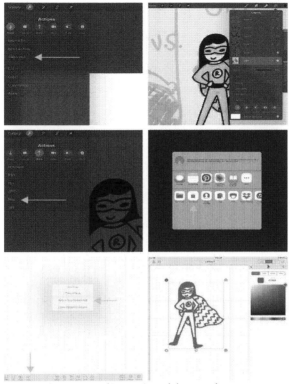

Photo credit- printablecrush.com

STEPS:

- The first thing to do is to convert your kid's drawing into an SVG file that Cricut Design Space recognizes. This will be done by tracing it in the ProCreate app.
- Get your child's design – it should not be too complex, to minimize weeding.
- Open the Procreate app on your iPad.
- Create a new canvas on ProCreate. Click on the wrench icon and select "IMAGE".
- Next, click "TAKE A PHOTO". Take a picture of the design. When you are satisfied with the image, click "Use it".
- On the Layer Panel (the two squares icon), add a new layer by clicking the plus sign.

- In the layers panel, select the layer containing the picture and click the N. Also, reduce the layer's opacity so that you can easily see your draw lines.
- From your imported brushes, select the Marker brush. To avoid the need to import a brush, choose the inking brush. You can resize the brush in the brush settings under the "General" option.
- On the new layer, trace over the drawing.
- Click on the wrench icon, click "Share", then "PNG".
- Next, save the image to your device.
- Alternately, use your black marker and trace the drawing on a blank piece of paper, then take a picture of it, using your iPad or phone.
- The next stage is to cut the design out in Cricut Design Space
- Open up the Cricut Design Space app on your iPad.
- Create a new project.
- Select "Upload" (located at the screen's bottom). Select "Select from Camera Roll" and select the PNG image you created in ProCreate or the image you traced out.
- Follow the next steps.
- Save the design as a cut file and insert it into the canvas. Here, you can resize the design or add other designs.
- Next, click "Make It" to send it to your Cricut.
- Choose "Vinyl" as the material.
- Place the vinyl on the mat and use the Cricut to cut it.
- Now, you can place the vinyl cutouts on the back to school supplies to make your child stand out!

CHAPTER FOUR

TIPS AND TECHINQUES

So far, so good! Are you feeling the flow of this book? Are you already benefiting from this book's information? Are you glad you found this book and can't wait to finish reading? I would be really happy if you left me your opinion on Amazon.

By now, I am certain that you are eager to go for any of the projects ideas listed above. However, you should not be in a hurry, this section will give you more insight and tips on how you can carry out those projects like a professional. Even if you know your way around the simple ones, you can still save much time, and reduce stress while on it. The Cricut Design Space has so many features that can only be used effectively if you know your way around them; you never know, that extra design that you would work hard to get done may have been achievable by a single click on a new feature. This section, therefore, is aimed at giving you advice about these.

The Cricut machine and software can indeed take a long time to master. But considering all the capabilities of both the machine (the vast number of materials it can work on) and the software (the unlimited number of designs that can be done on Cricut design space), it's safe to say that it's all worth the time and stress of learning. The design software is not as difficult as many people claim; it's just that the software environment needs to be explored on a serious level. The more you explore, the more you discover easier ways to design. Although it may look a little complicated at the beginning, you may even find the most elementary techniques a little bit difficult. Nevertheless, you will start getting used to the environment better when you start working on some projects discussed in previous sections. Be assured that the design space has everything you may need to craft remarkable projects. Moreover, there are several cool shortcuts that can make your work much faster and well-organized.

The tips and techniques about to be shared below are from experiences attained while working on the design space over time. Therefore, you should rest assured that this is the real deal, and not a bunch of redundant tips from a novice. Let's get on right with it.

To ensure clear communication, this section will be categorized into two parts;

Design Canvas platform - where various projects are created and where designs are modified.

Cut Screen platform – where settings are made on how materials are to be cut.

Design Canvas Platform

1. **Using Search Function Efficiently:** I have discovered that a lot of people underutilize the search feature in the design space image library. Although it might request for you to be a little more specific with your search terms, you just need the right keywords. Sometimes, a general term that is expected to produce all kinds of image results won't yield. However, changing a word or letter could suddenly yield more images. Therefore, it is reasonable to smartly continue trying many different search terms so as to discover the exact image you are looking for. To be clearer;

Refrain from using the "s" word: For example, if you search for "Dots" in the search field, you get nearly 115 images results. Then again, searching for the same word without the "s" will result in more than 200 images. So, if you want to get more image results while using the search function, it is advisable to refrain from using the "s: word.

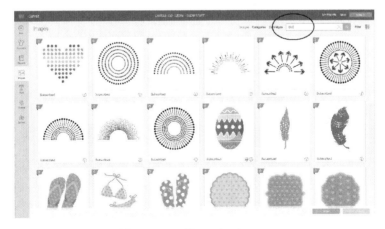

Photo credit- cricut.com

Use more synonym: Also, to get the best out of the search function, it is reasonable to look up image names by their synonyms. This is because every image is docketed with diverse search terms. If you want to cut labels, for instance, you should search for keywords such as circle, label, rectangle, square, or tag, to ensure that you get every possible image outcomes. The same goes for every other word synonyms; tags are very important.

2. **Tailor Your Project Designs with Slice, Contour, and Weld:** All images, regardless of where they originated from (whether the ones you uploaded by yourself or the ones you got from the image library), can be changed, modified, and personalized endlessly, making use of 3 primary editing tools; Slice, Counter, and Weld. You will find all these three tools at the lowermost right-side toolbar. These tools will highlight only when their functions are accessible for a particular design. At first, they may seem redundant as tools. Nevertheless, they are very resourceful and are exactly what you need to fully personalize your design. Find out more about these three tools deeply and utilize them maximally.

3. **Use Free Texts and Images:** A lot of people try to refrain from anything that requires them to pay before they can have access to it. However, if you're a dedicated crafter, you should definitely be an admirer of the Cricut access membership. Many individuals who are new to the Cricut system may, at first, not wish to spend their money simply to practice how to cut on their Cricut machines. But if you have just started learning about the whole system, really wish to personally see your Cricut machine working effectively, and, at the same time, save a lot of money on crafting

costs, then it is advisable to make use of the free resources provided within the Cricut design space.

To get free images: Make use of the "Filter" function within the design space image library. For example, just choose the option that says "Free", and it will display all the images you can utilize in your projects without paying any money.

Photo credit- cricut.com

To get free fonts: All Cricut machines are enabled to cut any type of font that is pre-installed on the computer. This is not limited to pre-installed fonts alone, it likewise cuts any font downloaded and installed on the computer by the user from free sites such as DaFont or Free Squirrel. If you want to look for fonts you can apply without incurring extra charges, you should make use of "My Fonts" that is located in the filter menu under "Fonts." This will display every available font that is installed on the computer, along with every Cricut font that you might have purchased through Cricut Access pass or from other sources. This proves to be an ideal way to make sure you're making use of fonts that won't cost you anything.

Photo credit- cricut.com

4. **Using Cartridge to Find Similar Images:** Sometimes, Cricut users get overwhelmed by the vast number of different image results they get whenever they search for an image in the design space image library. Whenever you search for an image, and you have too many different results, it's possible you spot a favorite one out of these images, and you may want more similar images. The best way to go about it is by making use of the particular cartridge (set) from which the image came from. The fastest and easiest way to access an image cartridge is by simply clicking on the tiny information icon (i) positioned at the lower right corner of that image in the design space image library. Doing that will reveal the details about the image, as well as a green link that gives you access to all the images of the same similarity. With this, you can start matching/coordinating images which is far better than the ones in search results.

Photo credit- cricut.com

5. **Color Management:** The Color Synchronization tool can save you a lot of time while working on projects. It also makes sure you're making use of matching colors across diverse designs. Most of the time, when working on many designs in the Design Canvas at once, you may wind up with numerous shades of identical colors. Rather than selecting every single layer independently to re-color, find your way to the color sync tool located at the right-hand side of the tool panel.

You'll only find the colors that are currently being used on your active project on this panel. However, you can likewise drag any active layer present on your design with your mouse and drop it in another color that has already been represented. If you wish to maintain identical colors all through your project designs or you want some layers to have a specific color so as to make your cutting efficient, using Color Sync is the easiest and fastest way to go about it.

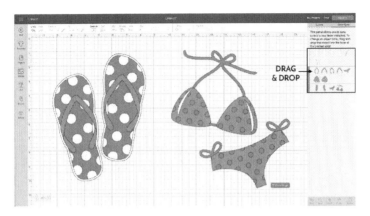

Photo credit- thehomesihavemade.com

6. **Cutting, Scoring, or Drawing Lines:** There was once a time when Cricut users have to look for designs with particular attributes to be able to draw or score (instead of cutting) a line. Well, those days are over. With the recent upgrade made on Cricut Design Space, you may now easily change any line from cut to draw to score by simply using the user-friendly Linetype menu located at the uppermost toolbar.

You will find that most of the designs will be tagged as "Cut" designs on your Design Space Canvas. However, you can effortlessly adjust the image outline to be scored (making use of the scoring wheel or scoring tool) or drawn (making use of pens). You just have to ensure that your design layers are not grouped or attached so as to change the way your project design will eventually be created.

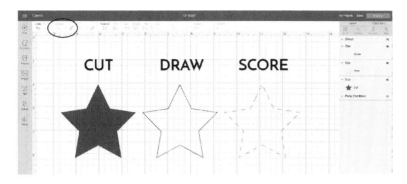

Photo credit- cricut.com

7. **Utilizing the Hide Tool:** When working on a project sometimes, you may find yourself filling up the Design space with lots of unnecessary images while experimenting, which, most of the time, leads to you cutting everything on the canvas when it's time to carve out your project. There are also times when you'll want or need to cut some parts of your design. Rather than deleting these redundant images off your canvas, you can hide them in a way by simply clicking on the eye icon beside the particular image on the Layers panel by the right-hand. Note that; any image that you hide will not be totally removed from the canvas. However, it won't be included with other images when you move your project away to cut it. You can toggle the "Hide" icon on or off. This makes it very easy to cut out only the parts you need and, at the same time, keep a clean and organized design canvas without losing track of those images you still wish to experiment on.

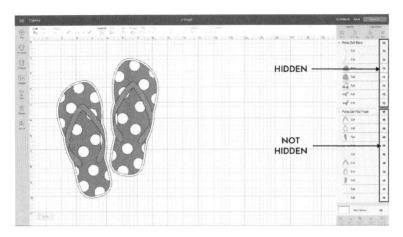

Photo credit- thehomesihavemade.com

8. **Modify Image Patterns:** The new "Fill" tool at the uppermost toolbar enables you to change how you fill your image. Selecting a single layer, you can switch colors or allot a different pattern to your image interior.

   There are several pre-loaded patterns you can fill your images with to make it more interesting without depending on cardstock or patterned scrapbook. Although there are several designs you can choose from, you can likewise alter the orientation and scale of the selected pattern by simply clicking on "Edit Pattern" under the pattern menu under "Fill" tab. However, you should also take note that this function can be used only through the Print-then-cut method.

9. **Using the Slice tool to Crop:** The "Crop" tool is a very popular tool available in almost all editing software. Unfortunately, this tool is not available on Cricut Design Space. A lot of Cricut users always wish they could have a Crop tool that allows them to easily and speedily slice through designs or filter out specific image details like they can in several other programs.

196

Nonetheless, you can easily carry out the same "Crop" function with the Slice tool together with the free-shapes, such as square, circle, etc., available in Cricut Design Space. It may feel a little bit tiresome at first, but you get used to it with practice.

10. **Using Keyboard Shortcuts:** Just like most Microsoft programs, Cricut Design Space has keyboard shortcuts for practically all the commands you can imagine, such as Cut, Copy, Paste, Delete, Duplicate, Undo, etc. You'll find these functions at every image corner, located at the uppermost toolbar in the Layers panel by the right-hand side. You can always save time by trying as many keyboard shortcuts as you can. You can try using working keyboard shortcuts from other computer software. Most of the shortcuts are generic; you can use "Control + C" to copy, "Control + X" to cut, "Control + V" to paste, "Control + Z" to undo, and so on.

Cut Screen Platform

Many Cricut users always think they can't do much editing on their projects after they are done with the designs and sending them for cutting through the "Make it" green button. However, there are so many things that can be done on the Cut screen platform that can not only save you some time, but also spare you some materials.

1. **Moving Images around a Single Mat:** Although the design space software automatically populates your images on the mat surface according to their orientation and color, it, oftentimes, doesn't arrange it the exact way you want your images to be. However, you can move these items around your mat while on the cut screen.

   To rearrange the way your items look like on the mat, all you have to do is drag and drop the images. You can even move and rotate a cut anyhow you want it on your mat. The rotation can be done by making use of the handles located at the topmost right-hand corner.

   Making these adjustments will not only enable you to make things more ideal than the software's default, it likewise makes sure that your cut is exactly where and how you want it. These adjustments will make it look good, especially if you are working on an oddly-shaped or scrap material. Just ensure that you fit your cut screen gridlines to your mat gridlines so as to make sure that the design matches the material accurately wherever you place it.

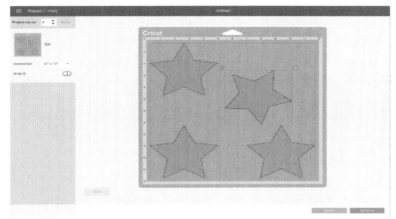

Photo credit- thehomesihavemade.com

2. **Moving Images from a Mat to Another:** Even though you can move your images around just one single mat, it is also possible to move your images from one mat to a different mat without needing to visit the Design Canvas and change the colors. You can do that by clicking on the three dots located at the topmost corner by the left-hand side of the image that is currently on the cut mat. After that, choose "Move to Another Mat." The design space will then enable you to select the mat you would like to put that particular image on. The change will be noticeable.

3.

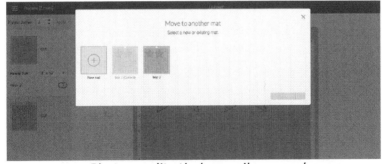

Photo credit- thehomesihavemade.com

You can make use of this feature any time you want to conserve your materials. And if you maneuver very well, you can fit more images on a single mat than the design space initially lays out. Also, this proves to be an ideal way of swiftly changing the color currently on any side of the design without needing to leave the cut screen and manually change the design's color.

4. **Re-cut or Skip Mats:** This remains one of the coolest features of Cricut Design Space. Much attention is not needed after sending your design for cutting. Provided that you feed your Cricut machine with the right paper size and color just as the cut screen displays it, your project will always come out exactly the way it was designed. Nevertheless, you may notice that you sometimes wish to re-cut a mat after the first time or skip the next mat in line. Fortunately, you can easily do that without even having to exit your cut screen.

Photo credit- thehomesihavemade.com

However, this must be done before your mat is loaded into the Cricut machine. You can choose a specific mat to cut next manually by simply clicking/selecting the mat on the cut screen by the left side. The cutting machine will automatically skip to the mat you manually.

Additionally, if you wish to re-cut a specific mat, even after there are cut-marks on it indicating that it has already been worked on, go back to the cut screen and choose the mat you wish to re-cut manually and the machine will automatically take care of the rest. However, you should be very careful whenever you skip or re-cut your mats. Make sure you always cross-check if what you are loading into your Cricut machine matches the highlighted mat on your cut screen. People slip up a lot when they skip or re-cut mats without paying close attention.

5. **Saving Commonly Used Materials:** A lot of users always feel shocked about how much they had missed whenever they discover this feature after a long time of using Cricut software! You are really missing a lot if you are not utilizing the "Custom materials" option.

Most people, especially individuals using the Cricut Explore Air 2 model, don't use this feature unknowingly because their machine is always set to Cardstock, Vinyl, Iron-in, and so on. Only Cricut Maker model users can easily notice the Custom materials option within the Cricut design space since there's no option to select the material you're cutting.

Photo credit- cricut.com

You can now stop going through the stress of browsing through over 200 custom material menu to get the same and common Cardstock, Iron-on, and Vinyl settings again and again. Just start adding all of them to the "Favorite" box! That's the trick! It will only take you some minutes to browse through the "Materials" menu and pinpoint the materials you use most frequently, click the star located under the "Materials" menu, then go on and choose "Favorites" rather than "Popular" on the same menu. All you will have left is a menu displaying every material you commonly cut. That's much more comfortable, right?

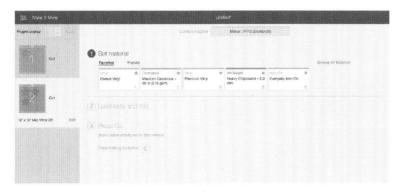

Photo credit- cricut.com

6. **Setting how to Cut Different Materials:** A lot of Cricut users often ask questions on how they can specifically adjust their materials cutting settings. For instance, some people set their machine to Vinyl and still complain that the machine doesn't cut through the material appropriately. Fortunately, you can modify the cut settings for any material from the "Materials" menu. You can set the blade, depth, number of passes, and so on.

To apply these settings on your cut screen, choose "Materials" option, or if you are not using Cricut Maker model, set your Cricut machine to Custom mode. After doing that, select "Browse All Materials", you'll find that at the top of the menu bar in green letters. You'll then find another link that says "Material Setting", also in green letters at the lowest part. When you have successfully made it to that point, you may now choose any material you want and start adjusting the settings as you would prefer it.

To avoid manual adjustments every time you discover that your machine is not cutting through your material appropriately, simply adjust the material settings once and for all.

7. **Connecting Two or More Cricut Machines Simultaneously:** Although the average Cricut user does not usually have above one Cricut machine, you can connect two or more machines to your Cricut design space account at once. This can be done either via USB or Bluetooth, on a wireless model. Also, you don't have to be worried about your designs and the machines getting mixed up when cutting. Regardless of the number of machines connected to your design space account, Cricut makes sure that the first step you perform on the concluding Cut Screen is to choose which one of your machines you would like to use for the cutting. This option will come in a dropdown menu at the top. This way, users can be sure they are making use of the intended Cricut machine all the time for their project.

8. **Easily Adjusting Cut Pressure:** Although it is amazing to be capable of adjusting the settings of your materials, all you need, sometimes, is a little extra or a lesser amount of pressure to get your machine to cut through your material efficiently. To adjust cut pressure, after selecting your choice material on the concluding Cut Screen, change the pressure through the provided dropdown menu. You can select the default pressure, increase or decrease it. Through this method, you can easily and quickly adjust the depth of your cutting without needing to mess around with the material's custom settings.

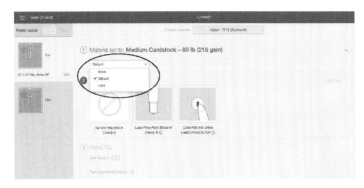

Photo credit- cricut.com

9. **Mirror Setting:** There are times when users need to cut their designs in reverse, especially when they're working with Iron-on projects. This reversing process is called "Mirror." Even though you can always flip your designs horizontally on your design canvas, there's an option available to mirror your designs while on the Cut Screen.

Doing this does not only allow you to "Mirror" the images/mats you wish to flip around, it likewise enables you to build and modify your design without flipping on the Design Canvas screen. This makes it more comfortable in view and customize.

Photo credit- thehomesihavemade.com

10. **Filling Your Mat by Adjusting Project Copies:** One of the features many Cricut users miss is the Auto-fill feature. Sadly, this feature is only available on the old Cricut machine models. With the old models, you can always put just one star on your design canvas, choose your paper size, and simply select "Auto-fill." On clicking "Auto-fill," the machine would automatically fill up your paper with stars, as many as could fit the paper comfortably. Although you won't find this same feature in the latest Design Space, there's a simple way you can work your way around it.

There's an option available at the topmost part of your cut screen immediately you enter the Cut Screen section where you can do your "Project Copies" settings. This function enables you to do your cutting as long as you wish on your Design Canvas. Even though it might take a few attempts before figuring out the number of copies that are needed to fill up your mat, it proves to be a faster solution than wasting of time duplicating on your Design Canvas.

11. **Following Reminder Instructions:** The invaluable reminders provided by the Design Space is among the top advantages of taking time to choose your custom materials while on the Cut Screen. This guarantees that your projects come out perfectly. For instance, whenever you choose "Iron-on" as a project material, reminders will be given to you to mirror your project designs and also place your Vinyl's gleaming side on the mat.

Photo credit- cricut.com

Also, whenever you choose a material like Chipboard, you will be prompted to confirm your blade is sharp and ready, place your material properly on your mat, and so on.

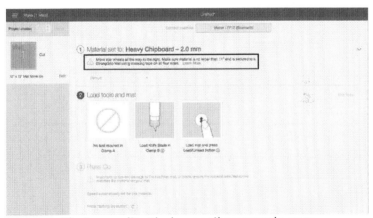

Photo credit- thehomesihavemade.com

You should not overlook these instructions because they look subtle; they are just measures of making sure you don't waste time or materials.

CONCLUSION

Using a Cricut machine should not be a new experience to you by now. However, it would be best if you kept an open mind to new updates. Cricut always give their users a lot of options to choose from, so, try as much as possible to carry out extensive research about their products, materials, and subscriptions.

At this stage, we can both agree that Cricut offers a whole lot more than it requires. Do not give up trying to learn how to cut on Cricut machines. Although it might be a little frustrating getting designs right sometimes, keep striving to attain perfection. You'll become professional in no time and probably start teaching other people how to use it.

Cricut machines are getting more popular every day. A lot of people have a preference for Cricut machines for many reasons. Some of the reasons are;

User-Friendliness: This is one of the major reasons that people choose Cricut machines to do their cutting job. It's easy to use and also easy to learn if you have the right resources. Almost anyone can set up a Cricut machine because it is not too complicated. All that a new user has to do is to follow the straightforward instructions that come with the box.

Attractiveness: A lot of individuals like having their gadgets come in cool designs and structure. Cricut machines check this box emphatically, coming with very attractive designs and appearance.

Flexibility: Cricut machines are designed to handle multipurpose tasks. A lot of work can be done on it without stress. You can write, score, and cut with the machine. A lot of Cricut users are yet to reach the maximum level usage. With Cricut, people rarely over-utilize, most people only underutilize.

Apart from these three main advantages, you can also gain easy accessibility to Cricut machines and have no need to download software. As you continue to use this platform, you get more attached to it; it's only normal.

So, the book ends here. If you've mastered every tip and technique in this book, congratulations! You've just become a professional Cricut user! However, it would help if you did not forget the most important things discussed in this book. If you forget things quickly, have this book with you every time you want to work on your Cricut machine. If you liked this book and it has helped you in many ways to build your Cricut skill, then kindly let me know your opinion on Amazon. You can also recommend this book to your friends that are new or having issues with Cricut machines. The power of creation now lies in your hands, literally! Godspeed!

Printed by Amazon Italia Logistica S.r.l.
Torrazza Piemonte (TO), Italy

12613862R00121